D1474794

Judicial Misconduct

Judicial Misconduct
A Cross-National Comparison

by *Mary L. Volcansek*

with

Maria Elisabetta de Franciscis
Università di Napoli, Federico II

and

Jacqueline Lucienne Lafon
Université de Paris, XI

K
2146
.V648
1996
West

University Press of Florida
Gainesville / Tallahassee / Tampa / Boca Raton
Pensacola / Orlando / Miami / Jacksonville

Copyright 1996 by the Board of Regents of the State of Florida
Printed in the United States of America on acid-free paper ∞
All rights reserved

01 00 99 98 97 96 6 5 4 3 2 1

Library of Congress Cataloging-in-Publication Data

Volcansek, Mary L., 1948–
    Judicial misconduct: a cross-national comparison / by Mary L. Volcansek with
Maria Elisabetta de Franciscis and Jacqueline Lucienne Lafon.
        p. cm.
    Includes bibliographical references and index.
    ISBN 0-8130-1421-2 (alk. paper)
        1. Judicial corruption—United States.   2. Disqualification of judges—United
States.   3. Judicial corruption—Great Britain.   4. Disqualification of judges—Great
Britain.   5. Judicial corruption—France.   6. Disqualification of judges—France.
7. Judicial corruption—Italy.   8. Disqualification of judges—Italy.   I. De Franciscis,
Maria Elisabetta, 1956–.   II. Lafon, Jacqueline Lucienne.   III. Title.
K2146.V648   1996   95-19568
347'.014—dc20   CIP
[342.714]

The University Press of Florida is the scholarly publishing agency for the State Univer-
sity System of Florida, comprised of Florida A & M University, Florida Atlantic Univer-
sity, Florida International University, Florida State University, University of Central
Florida, University of Florida, University of North Florida, University of South Florida,
and University of West Florida.

University Press of Florida
15 Northwest 15th Street
Gainesville, FL 32611

For Harry

Contents

Preface

This book emerged from my interest in how "bad" judges can be removed from their positions. As I learned more about the processes in the United States, my curiosity about other systems increased, and I invited my colleagues Elisabetta de Franciscis and Jacqueline Lafon to join me in a comparative study. Each contributed a chapter to the project, on Italy and France, respectively. Professor Lafon suggested that Britain should be included for the sake of symmetry, and I am grateful for her recommendation because it led me to a deeper understanding of the English judicial system.

There are a number of people who contributed to the completion of this book. I wish to thank Eduardo Gamarra, Donald W. Jackson, and Martin Edelman for their careful readings of the manuscript and useful suggestions for its improvement. Russ Wheeler of the Federal Judicial Center was, as always, helpful in providing information, and Cindy Gray, director of the Center for Judicial Conduct Organizations of the American Judicature Society, was most cooperative with data on the work of judicial conduct organizations. Professor Lafon wishes to acknowledge the assistance of Bernard Darcos of the French Ministry of Justice, who gave her access to discipline records. John Stack and Walda Metcalf both provided encouragement throughout, for which I am most grateful. I also owe a debt of thanks to Dorinda Mosby, who helped me conquer the computer when necessary. My greatest appreciation, though, is reserved for my husband, Harry Antrim, who read and commented on countless versions of the manuscript. Whatever errors remain are, of course, my responsibility.

Chapter 1

Judges and Democracy

The term *democracy* literally means power (*kratos*) and people (*demos*), but the direct translation to "power of the people" is a far more complicated matter both in theory and in practice. A minimal definition is that offered by Dahl—"the processes by which ordinary citizens exert a relatively high degree of control over leaders."[1] Judiciaries are common institutions in democracies and authoritarian regimes alike, but with the exception of those few jurisdictions that use elections to name people to courts there is no direct way for citizens to control judges or to hold them accountable. Those who wield the judicial power are consequently anomalies in democracies. Most democratic theorists have chosen to ignore this inconsistency, but politicians have certainly recognized the aberrant nature of the judicial beast. The specter of a *gouvernement des juges* is often invoked in Europe, and members of the 1947 Italian Constitutional Convention even remarked on the frustration of democratic will and New Deal legislation by the U.S. Supreme Court.[2] The issue of judicial accountability in democracies is a critical, though often neglected, force in achieving or maintaining democracy.

Most considerations of judicial accountability have focused on the recruitment and selection of judges. This volume addresses the question from the opposite direction, from the perspective of the discipline and removal of errant judges. Judges are human and make errors, and for criminal conduct, presumably, they can be punished like other people. Moreover, there is ordinarily a more exacting standard of behavior expected of

1

judges, because of the power they can exert over liberty and property. When they fail, though, how can or how does the political system respond? When they become disabled by virtue of physical or mental infirmity, is there a means for protecting litigants?

There are three basic prototypes for sanctioning judicial misbehavior in Western democracies: the English system, in which discipline is the prerogative of Parliament; the French civil service model, in which judges, together with the minister of justice, largely police their own ranks; and the practice in some American states whereby the electorate holds the power of removal. Of these, only the last is clearly consistent with generally held notions of democracy, but it is frequently criticized as being ineffective (as will be discussed in chapter 5), and it rather obviously clashes with another cherished value, judicial independence.

Judicial independence was practiced in France under the Ancien Régime, where judges by virtue of having bought their offices were not beholden to the monarch. And it was the Frenchman Montesquieu who in 1748 provided the justification for a separate and insular judiciary: "There is no liberty, if the judiciary power be not separated from the legislative and the executive."[3] The often repeated logic of seeking an impartial third party to resolve disputes when the competing interests cannot is the common sense rationale for judicial independence.[4] Montesquieuian independence from other powers of government, however, is a matter distinct from the impartiality of the judge in a given case.[5] Even though judicial independence within a structure of government may be less common in the world as a whole, it is generally regarded in Western democracies as an essential element in the definition of judging. As Becker put it, impartiality, objectivity, or detachment forms one criterion for a court and political independence yet another.[6] The link between an independent judiciary and the protection of individual rights has become so widely accepted that the United Nations Commission on Human Rights, at a congress of one of its subagencies in 1988, adopted a statement requiring that "the independence of the judiciary shall be guaranteed by the State and enshrined in the Constitution or law of the country."[7] The tension that exists between judicial accountability and judicial independence is largely ignored except in debates over how to recruit judges, and in that context it is complicated by the necessity of ensuring some measure of technical or professional competence.[8]

Removal or discipline of judges is generally neglected in discussions of selection mechanisms and certainly in writings about democracy and democratization. This book is intended as a step toward filling that void by comparing the historical evolution of the English system, whereby Parliament holds the power of removal, and of the French civil service model, in which judges participate in the policing of their own number. I will also trace the transplantation and adaptation of these two systems in other national cultures. The English tradition traveled to the United States, and the French practice was adopted in Italy in 1907. The electoral system that developed and remains in use in some American states will also be included, though it notably has not been imitated elsewhere. History provides a backdrop and culture sets the stage, but how each system currently functions and is capable of deflecting fears stemming from the undemocratic nature of the judiciary are matters of primary importance.

Judges and Political Power

Standard assumptions behind the exclusion of courts and judges from discussions of democratic accountability are the beliefs that judicial offices are apolitical, that judges have no discretion and are merely *la bouche de la loi* (the mouth of the law), and that judges simply apply or interpret but do not make law. These myths have been largely debunked in the United States since the advent of the legal realist movement, and volumes, both theoretical and empirical, have been written to demonstrate the political nature of courts. Outside academic circles in Europe, however, the notions continue to be more or less perpetuated. To do otherwise would be to deny two basic axioms that underlie parliamentary democracy: parliamentary sovereignty and the passive nature of the judicial role—that is, the judge "may declare the law but not create it."[9]

Where judicial review is exercised, however, such denials are transparently fallacious. If judges may veto laws passed by the legislature, then there clearly is a judicial power. France recognized this link as early as 1790, when the National Assembly passed a law stating, "The courts cannot take any part, directly or indirectly, in the exercise of the legislative power nor prevent or postpone the execution of the decrees of the legislative body."[10] The essentially countermajoritarian nature of judicial review has fueled a lively intellectual debate, particularly in the United States, where the constitutional basis of such a power is only implicit. The essence of that exchange, stated succinctly, concerns how to validate the actions of undemocratically selected judges who can block laws enacted by a democratically elected legislature.

The debate that has been rekindled in the last decade in constitutional law circles is actually not new; it is a relabeled version of an ongoing dialogue between positivism and natural law,[11] Jeffersonian versus Hamiltonian views,[12] originalists and nonoriginalists,[13] or more recently between interpretivists and noninterpretivists.[14] The lengthy verbiage can all be reduced to an attempt to "reconcile the countermajoritarian practice of judicial review with the majoritarian structure of our representative democracy,"[15] and is, according to Tushnet, "just constitutional law's version of the general crisis of legitimacy."[16] The amount of scholarly attention that attempts to distinguish correct or appropriate uses of judicial review from wrong or inappropriate applications of the power simply underscores the awareness, at least in the legal community, of the paradox.

Not surprisingly, therefore, European nations with their strong belief in parliamentary sovereignty resisted adoption of any form of judicial review. The Fascist and Nazi experiences, however, changed that inclination,[17] and judicial review was introduced into Germany and Italy and later into France and Spain. By 1989, prior to the founding of new democracies, 65 nations had adopted judicial review in some form.[18] The rationale behind the widespread acceptance of this judicial power is likely the same as what motivated the founders in the United States: the fear of legislative tyranny outweighs apprehensions of judicial despotism.[19] An intrinsically undemocratic institution is thus accepted almost uncritically. The justification offered is that "the policy views in the Court are never for long out of line with the policy views dominant among law-making majorities of the United States."[20] A similar explanation has been offered for the German Federal Republic[21] and for implementation of the Charter of Rights in Canada.[22] The validity of that assertion is not universally accepted, but where judicial review has been given to courts the judiciary clearly entered the political fray. The U.S. Supreme Court has voided hundreds of state laws, but only 140 national statutes have been invalidated. The newer constitutional tribunals in Western Europe have been notably more active than their North American counterparts. The Italian Constitutional Court, for example, dismantled much of the Fascist security law and reordered church-state relations, and the German and French bodies have been central in fashioning the laws on press pluralism and electoral reform.

Judicial review is the most visible exertion of judicial power, but it is hardly the only one. Its relevance is, moreover, diminished in our discussion of judicial accountability since in both France and Italy judicial review is restricted to a single body that is separate from the judiciary, per se; in Britain parliamentary sovereignty prohibits the practice; and in the United States, though judicial review is decentralized and in theory can be exercised by any court, only the Supreme Court has the ultimate say. Only one justice of that court, in more than 200 years, has been the subject of a serious attempt at removal. There is an additional limitation in the scope of this work that should be noted at the outset. Most of the judiciaries that follow the French model, including those of Italy and most of the rest of continental Europe, are made up of two divisions. The ordinary courts handle typical criminal and civil litigation. Napoleon in 1799 separated administrative courts from the ordinary ones and granted to them exclusive authority to review executive and administrative actions. In the French case there are also the specialized commercial courts.[23] This specialization has been followed in a number of countries and even extended in other nations, most notably in the Federal Republic of Germany, where there are four distinct divisions of courts in addition to the ordinary judiciary and the Constitutional Court. Because of the specific character of administrative courts in both France and Italy, they are not included in this book.

All societies need rule-adjudication.[24] Or, as Shapiro says, courts are necessarily involved in conflict resolution and social control. Friction is generated when courts exercise discretion (and there is always the possibility of a judge's deciding among competing facts or from among competing norms in any given case); in such situations there is some kind of "supplementary and interstitial" law-making occurring. It is particularly true in common law countries where much of the law is essentially judge-made.[25] The term *common law* connotes judicial participation in policy-making, at least to the extent of judges filling lacunae in statutes. The judicial role in application of legislative pronouncements has been likened to that of musical performers in interpreting the work of a composer.[26] It is necessary because statutes are often ambiguously worded or fail to address all of the myriad situations of fact that may arise.[27] Judges are, moreover, frequently called upon to choose among competing norms or to decide a case for which there is no applicable statute. The system, though it originated in England, can be found in various guises in the nations that were British colonies.

The British deny courts the power of judicial review, insofar as that means invalidating parliamentary enactments. Blackstone in 1765, relying on the writings of Sir Edward Coke, declared Parliament to be omnipotent: "It hath sovereign and uncontrollable authority in the making, confirming, enlarging, restraining, abrogating, repealing, reviving and expounding of laws, concerning all matters of possible denominations, ecclesiastical or temporal, civil, military, maritime or criminal. . . . True it is, that what the parliament doth, no authority upon earth can undo."[28] That statement was echoed more than a century later by Bagehot, who claimed there is virtually no topic, large or small, that "a new House of Commons can[not] despotically and finally resolve."[29] It remains equally true today. In an interesting historical irony, Coke, the often quoted authority for the preeminence of Parliament, claimed in his capacity as a judge in *Dr. Bonham's Case* in 1606 that according to many cases in the common law a higher authority, "common right or reason," can "controul acts of parliament and sometimes adjudge them to be utterly void."[30]

Courts in England continue to be viewed largely as apolitical, lacking significant political power. Judicial intrusion into political matters is denied because of political and legal cultures, the primacy of positivism in English jurisprudence, and an adherence to a tradition that tends to characterize both the legal and judicial fields. Nonetheless, torts, contracts, property, wills, and criminal procedure in England, Wales, and Northern Ireland are areas of law that are largely the creation of judges through the common law.[31] "The rationale of judicial subordination," Gavin Drewry suggests, "quickly crumbles at the edges when exposed to daylight."[32]

Even Lord Devlin, when Master of the Rolls, implied that English courts are "activist" to the extent that they are "keeping pace with consensus," or are "dynamic" or "creative" in their law-making, or are attempting "to generate change in the consensus."[33] This trend can be most readily seen in the use of judicial review, a term in English law that refers not to reviewing statutes for constitutionality but rather to an "instrument of administrative law, encompassing a cluster of remedies available in the courts for challenging the legality or fairness of acts or omissions by public authorities."[34] The courts in this context have affected transportation policies and educational reform, doing what Drewry calls "patrolling the boundaries." Moreover, Britain's membership in the European Union has even caused a parliamentary act to be voided by the courts because it was contrary to the treaties, and the political role of judges would be increased even further if the European Convention in Human Rights were to be enacted into domestic law.[35]

Common law as practiced in other nations is typically less restrained by tradition and is bolstered by the requirement of a federal arbiter, as in Canada, or by the existence of a rigid constitution. The Canadian experience is probably among those closest to British traditions. Canada's first constitutional document, the 1867 British North America Act, retained the primacy of Parliament and denied courts the power to review legislation, but the federal character of Canada required that courts be able, when there was a clear usurpation of power, to referee between the national and provincial governments.[36] Even when judges were merely applying or interpreting the law, they still retained "plenty of room to maneuvre."[37] The 1982 Charter of Rights broadened the scope of judicial action and has meant that "more and more political issues will be subjected to this peculiarly legal form of resolution."[38]

The Australian experience diverges, but in its case there was a conscious effort to model the judiciary not along English lines but in imitation of the United States. The judiciary is a separate branch of government, and the High Court of Australia is explicitly granted the power of judicial review. Using that authority the High Court has played an important role in "reshaping the constitutional powers of government"[39] and has even intervened in cabinet secrecy and privilege by determining what documents may be shielded by the executive from court proceedings.[40]

Indian practices, on the other hand, seem to illustrate the truism that similar institutions, sharing the same roots, grow quite differently when grafted onto different cultures. Building on the practice of the Raj between 1937 and 1950, when only limited judicial review was granted to the Federal Court, Indian independence brought a new constitution that granted the judiciary five high-prerogative writs. When the judiciary promptly invalidated a number of laws, the constitution was amended, "again and again culminating in the famous 'amendment' during the [1973] emergency."[41] The judges' resort to administrative judicial review has been met with parliament's progressive restriction of judges' power.[42]

The United States is, of course, typically cited as the prime example of the common law's lending itself to the exercise of judicial power. Because of judicial review, "American politics have been notably Constitution centered."[43] But even beyond the realm of judicial review, U.S. courts are generally recognized as being involved in policy-making to the extent that through the American version of common law they establish and apply authoritative rules. This process is implicit in dispute resolution, social control, and assignment of wins and losses.[44] Courts in the common law tradition, in short, participate in varying measures in the political process. The determination of politicians in India to curtail the power of the judiciary dramatically attests to this fact.

The basic premises that drive the civil law tradition include a determination to circumscribe the potential for judicial meddling in political matters. Codes were written that in theory required nothing more of a judge than to apply the law; they were expected to be comprehensive and leave nothing to the discretion of the judge. Courts were forbidden to intrude upon the legislative arena and were, at least in the abstract, denied "even such interstitial creativity as is required by the interpretation of statutes"; they were the mouth but not the brains of the law.[45] Though it has antecedents in Roman law, modern code law dates from Napoleon's restructuring of the French judiciary and his desire to systematize the law. Five codes were written under his direction: Civil Code (1804), Commercial Code (1807), Code of Civil Procedure (1807), Code of Criminal Instruction (1809), and Penal Code (1810). Judicially created jurisprudence was denied, for if it were admitted, the argument went, "different initiatives could rise from one or other jurisdiction, and there should be an effort of harmonization."[46] French codes were imitated by the German Civil Code of 1900 and the Swiss Code of 1907. Versions of the French codes were also introduced in Belgium, the Netherlands, and Italy.

Despite the intentions behind the codes to block judicial creativity, judges in virtually every continental country still must interpret the rules; "the code was not and could not be the whole body of legal rules."[47] Even those who wrote the French civil code knew that it was impossible to cover every contingency with an applicable rule and decided instead "to give the judge a general frame, the main principles, which would serve as reference and enable him to solve the case."[48] The result of that judicial creativity is reflected in the French civil and administrative codes and is found also in the work of other civil law judges. Dutch judges, although also governed by codes and lacking the power to rule on the constitutionality of legislation, have on a case-by-case basis significantly influenced the law on labor strikes, abortion, and euthanasia.[49] Likewise, Belgian judges through resort to purposive or teleological interpretations have affected public policies on morals, human rights, linguistic freedoms, refugees, and economics.[50]

Working with common law or code law, with or without the power of judicial review, judges indeed influence national policy and are, thereby, participants in the national power structure. The methods, techniques, or styles of interpretation may vary from nation to nation and from culture to culture, but the outcomes appear similar. When a court or courts have the power to review legislation, the political nature of judges is most obvious, but it flourishes also in less overt forms in other contexts. This recognition marks the inconsistency that judges represent in democratic polities.

Judicial Independence

Since judges wield some type of political power in democratic societies, judicial independence compounds the undemocratic character of the judiciary. In fact, one of the precepts that is most widely cited as undergirding judicial legitimacy is the requirement that judges be seen as independent. So high, indeed, is the premium placed on maintaining the appearance of judicial independence that authoritarian regimes, for example, Zia's in Pakistan, Marcos's in the Philippines, and Indira Gandhi's in India during her emergency era, all either refrained from publicly attacking the judicial system or resorted to subterfuges to coerce acquiescence from the courts.[51]

Independence for the judiciary is usually justified as a rationalization for substituting coercion for consent.[52] The assumption is that fairer hearings will result from an institution that is separated from the legislative and executive branches, but it is a premise that remains untested.[53] There is, moreover, confusion as to exactly what constitutes independence. Schmidhauser defines it as "the possession of some degree of freedom from one or more competing branches of government or from the centers of private power."[54] Becker breaks the notion into more specific elements: (1) the belief of a judge that he can act on his own, (2) counter to what others, political or judicial, may think, (3) particularly when there is a possibility of retribution, either personal or institutional.[55]

Judicial independence is not a simple absolute, either present or absent. It is, rather, a matter of degree, a question of shading. U.S. federal judges come extremely close to absolute independence, since their tenure is for life and their salaries cannot be diminished. In more than 200 years, only seven have been removed from office. At the other end of the spectrum, Bolivian judges are clearly not independent. Although all Bolivian constitutions have asserted a commitment to judicial independence, since 1936 there have been 16 purges of the judiciary for purposes of "renovation."[56] Between those two poles lies an almost infinite number of possibilities for interference and for autonomy.

Formal mechanisms to ensure independence normally include lengthy and secure tenure and adequate salary. However, there are a number of informal ties that may diminish or foster independent action, even where the formal rules seem clearly designed to insulate judicial personnel from outside pressures.

The connection of a judge to the appointing authority is an obvious one. It is no secret that U.S. presidents make a concerted attempt to name individuals to the federal bench who they believe share their ideologies. The process for naming judges to the German Constitutional Court is also highly politicized.[57] There are strict party quotas, and in some areas of law party affiliation has been found to be a factor in the judges' voting.[58] Appointments to the French Constitutional Council are governed primarily by party affiliation, and its ranks have been filled mostly by professional politicians.[59] In Italy the judges of the Constitutional Court are also named partly according to party allotment, and not only do sitting ministers of justice win appointments to that body but former presidents of the court move into the cabinet upon completion of their nine-year, nonrenewable terms. This has been the case at least with former presidents Paladin, La Pergola, and Conso. Appointers can use their power to name judges for reasons of patronage or partisan politics and also to achieve particular ethnic, regional, or gender goals.

Other, more subtle influences may bias judges and intrude upon their independence. More than one commentator has noted the essentially conservative nature of judges, by virtue of their socioeconomic backgrounds and education, and their propensity to support and protect the status quo.[60] This tendency is demonstrated in Britain, at least in the view of Labour Party leaders who believe that the courts have actively intervened to limit the political activity and power of trade unions.[61] Ironically, because of guarantees of judicial independence, judges are likewise more free to innovate and promote political and social change.[62]

The French civil service model for the ordinary courts was designed to overcome influences emanating from the appointer. Although the president of the republic remains the tacit nominator of all magistrates, actual selection of judges is based on examinations, training, and the recommendation of the Superior Council of the Magistrature and the minister of justice.[63] That process is replicated in Italy and in many of the other continental countries. In Italy, however, magistrates are not prohibited from assuming other positions in the executive branch, in Parliament, or in other government divisions; so long as they take temporary leave from their judicial tasks, neither place nor seniority are affected.[64]

Independence for judges should not be confused with absolute autonomy in all contexts. Even where judges are unremovable, as in France, there are limits. In May 1832, André Marie Dupin, the famous head of the prosecution department assigned to the Cour de Cassation, noted that a judge may not, despite having security in office, act with impunity.[65] The same sentiment was restated in the 1980s by U.S. District Judge Gerhardt Gessell, who said that a judge must not "confuse independence of the judiciary with his desire for unbridled personal independence."[66] Though there may be independence, it is not without boundaries. Judges are, in fact, usually expected to surpass the standards of ethical behavior that attach to other political officeholders. They are to be, like Caesar's wife, above reproach. Actions that might be wholly acceptable for a legislator or a cabinet minister would raise eyebrows if undertaken by a judge. Moreover, an ethical lapse by a judge can have repercussions quite disproportionate to the "sin." Public opinion may likewise demand greater punishment for a miscreant judge than for a politician or, certainly, for the ordinary citizen. Political independence of the institution is clearly an attribute separable from the personal independence of any judge that is essential for impartial adjudication of an individual case. The bounds placed on personal behavior are generally stringent to ensure that impartiality prevails.

Democratic Theory and Judicial Power

If, as I have said, judges are players in the political game even to the limited extent of giving life to statutes and codes through interpretation and application in concrete cases, they are participants in allocating political power. Wherever they exercise judicial review, that participation is not even questionable. Therefore, following the simple and relatively comprehensive definition of democracy offered by Dahl in 1956, there should be some process or processes "by which ordinary people exert a relatively high degree of control over" political officials, including judges.[67] Or, as Schmitter and Karl phrased it, "political democracy is a system of governance in which rulers are held accountable for their actions in the public realm by citizens, acting indirectly through the competition and cooperation of their elected representatives."[68] That sense of accountability is, at least on the face of it, counter to the judicial independence that some, like Olson, see as an essential ingredient for a lasting democracy.[69] That's the rub.

How has this contradiction been addressed? The simple answer is that most democratic theorists have chosen to ignore it, but that response obscures some attempts at reconciliation and some of the more subtle yet important aspects of the issue. Democracy and democratization have become favored subjects for theorists and for comparativists, first in the aftermath of World War II and again with the third wave of democratization that began in 1974. What is strikingly apparent, first, is the absence of an agreed-upon definition of "democracy." Sartori, for example, concludes that the three crucial elements on which contemporary democracies hinge are elective procedures, limited majority rule, and the representational transmission of power.[70] Laurence Whitehead adds to that description by emphasizing "electoral competition among freely constituted political parties" and "classical liberal guarantees of individual freedom."[71] Guarantees for individual or minority rights (the limit that Sartori places on majority rule)[72] are typically recognized, but precisely how to achieve or protect them in democracies is left vague. Those of us who study law and courts immediately recognize, in the tradition of Montesquieu, that courts, constitutions, and constitutional traditions are the relevant government institutions because they are not empowered by the whim of public sentiment but rather stand as the bulwark between the tyranny of the majority and the rights of the individual. Lijphart acknowledges the role of a court with the power of judicial review as one possible restraint on parliamentary majorities, but he also concedes that many nations reject that formulation in favor of representative democratic control of constitutionality.[73]

The literature addressing democracy is vast and falls into two broad categories. Some, like Sartori, Dahl, and Lijphart, focus on defining democracy and ascertaining the conditions that sustain or inhibit it. Others concentrate on "democratization," or the process by which authoritarian regimes are transformed into democratic ones. The judicial function is not treated, generally speaking, as an element worthy of comment either in the transition to or the maintenance of democracies. Indeed, meager attention is paid to institutional factors at all. Parties and party systems are the focus of some work,[74] as is the role of constitutional opposition.[75] Przeworski is among the few who see the value of institutions. In the transformation process, he proposes that the "solution to the democratic compromise consists of institutions" that can limit uncertainties and lessen the threats to those who might still be able to block democratization.[76] The role of courts, judges, or legal traditions otherwise passes without comment.[77] Even when Diamond addresses the paradoxes of democracy—conflict versus consensus, representativeness versus governability, and consent versus effectiveness—the judicial anomaly is missed.[78] This omission seems odd in light of the so-called new institutionalism[79] that seeks a "dialectic of meaningful actions and structural determinants."[80] That approach recognizes that "the institutions of law and bureaucracy occupy a dominant role in contemporary life."[81] Or, put differently, "humans propose, structures dispose."[82]

When the judiciary is recognized, it is often treated pejoratively. Linz, for example, cites the tendency when there is a loss of coalition cohesion to transform political issues into legal ones; the strategy is to buy time through the infamously slow legal process. He points more specifically, though, to the doubtful "legitimacy of having judicial bodies make what are essentially political decisions in a democracy."[83] Linz's remark is hardly novel; each alternative strategy he pursues is also acknowledged to be counter to democratic authenticity. His comments relate strictly to challenges of the constitutional sort. Sartori poses, from a different perspective, the judicial power question in the broader context of judges abdicating their role as law-finders and shifting more to one of "judge/legislator" and "increasingly tak[ing] the law in their hand as if there was nothing more to it than having a winning hand."[84] His solution is increased reliance on rigid constitutions that are not easily altered by judicial fiat. Taken together, the Linz and Sartori approaches point to a dilemma of democracy, if we can trust neither the judges nor the legislators with the constitution.

Not all who have pondered the processes of democracy have ignored judicial power. Both Dahl and Bobbio have tried to rationalize the judicial role in a democratic government. Bobbio's solution is to differentiate among types of law and between different law-makers. He distinguishes between government *sub lege* (under law), which occurs when the judge makes a specific and concrete decision, and government *per leges* (via law), which is seen when the first legislator draws a law. Government *sub lege* is essential to preventing the abuse of power, whereas the motive for *per leges* is to create the written constitution that demarcates the boundaries.[85] That distinction may be useful in an abstract sense, but it offers little guidance about democratic control of judges who may claim to decide *sub lege* but who may indeed abuse *per leges*.

Dahl begins with the more useful proposition that "'democracies' are never fully democratic: they invariably fall short of democratic criteria in some respects."[86] He conceives of judges as among those undemocratic elements but as a reasonable alternative if fundamental rights cannot be protected through democratic means. Judges, then, are "quasi-guardians," making "their decisions within the context of a generally democratic system" but one not "democratically controlled."[87] However, Dahl limits his discussion to situations in which judicial review is practiced and adds that there must be an inverse relationship between the authority of the judges and the authority of the democratically selected leaders, because there is no evidence that fundamental rights are better protected with quasi guardians than without them. A principal justification he offers is that judges are not long out of line with the elected law-making majorities. Even so, where a polity has opted for quasi-guardian judges, Dahl points to the need to restrict severely the scope of their authority.[88] Dahl's conception falls short only to the extent that it avoids the more common complaints about judges as guardians who make concrete decisions that are separate and distinct from questions of constitutionality but that remain, nonetheless, political.

Dahl's and Bobbio's analyses lead back to the debates among constitutional scholars over correct versus incorrect uses of judicial review, and they fail to shed much light on the basic constraints on judges using their discretion to fashion political or politically relevant decisions, distinct from issues of constitutionality. Guarnieri has offered a useful fourfold typology for classifying judges with reference to their political autonomy and judicial creativity that recognizes the spectrum of judicial authority. Where autonomy is high, but creativity is limited, he borrows Dahl's terminology of guardian judge, who uses the judicial power to ensure the fundamental rights of the citizen. Where autonomy and creativity are both high, he calls the judge political. In this instance the judge uses discretion to reach political conclusions that make policy and that may go beyond what the case requires. Where autonomy is low but creativity high, he places the delegate judge. This judge is the representative of the political community and uses general clauses in the law to find politically acceptable solutions. This judge's creativity is interstitial. Finally, the least problematic is the executor judge, who has low autonomy and low creativity. This is the judge who is passive and faithful to the command of the legislature, who declares the law.[89] The limitations that Guarnieri envisions as preventing abuse of power by the judiciary are public opinion, collegial courts, the appellate process, and, most important, self-restraint.[90] He concludes, even so, that there is no single optimal means for resolution of the tension between democratic norms and judicial power.[91]

I agree to a large extent with Guarnieri on the absence of one overarching solution to the predicament. I do see, however, some clues at the theoretical level. Sartori offers a relevant distinction between *politics* and *politicization* in discussing all realms of democratic life. This differential is useful if politics is simply the exertion of political power and if politicization refers to use of that power for partisan ends. Judiciaries are political, but they can behave apolitically. Sartori sees politics, even in its mildest forms, as destructive when it permeates the judiciary, military, civil service, or higher education.[92] Keeping the judiciary unpoliticized may be possible through the means listed by Guarnieri, but it can also be achieved through a recognition that the political control granted to any elite in democracies "is always temporary and always conditional."[93]

The accountability that attaches to judges extends beyond responsibility for the correctness of judicial decisions. The appeals process is, in fact, the mechanism that is generally relied upon to rectify any failure in application of law or determination of fact. Public expectations normally hold that judges are otherwise responsible for actions that may call their impartiality into question. Cappelletti surveyed various schemes used to secure judicial responsibility and created a fourfold taxonomy for classification of judges' accountability: political accountability for judges individually and for the institution that includes some liability to the political branches or to the constitution; societal or public accountability; vicarious legal accountability of the state for judicial errors; and personal legal accountability that may be criminal, civil, or disciplinary.[94] Societal and political accountability are the forms most directly tied to questions of judicial power and democracy, but legal responsibility is more than tangentially related. The goal of making the judicial office temporary and conditional in democratic polities subsumes the possibility of correcting and punishing misbehavior.

In short, judicial accountability must be understood in a democratic context as the element that makes the power of any judge potentially temporary and always conditional. Continuance in office must be predicated on ethical and nonpoliticized actions. A judge's tenure is limited by the requirement that decisions be made impartially, objectively, and conscientiously and be made free from tainted influences or from a political bias. Those criteria do not infringe upon the essential qualities of institutional independence or freedom of decision. That distinction, so alarmingly simple, is at the same time excruciatingly difficult to apply in a concrete case of alleged misbehavior. The judge can always claim persecution for exercising independence and try to shift the guilt of politicization to the accusers. But, if those who sit on the bench can use incomplete or unclear evidence to decide the guilt or innocence of those accused of crimes and to assign culpability in civil litigation, somebody must also be equally capable of assessing the fitness of a judge to sit in judgment over others.

Cross-National Comparisons

With contributions from my European colleagues, I now offer a comparison of how four different nations have fashioned systems to address judicial accountability. The logic of the comparative approach seems self-evident, but the pitfalls that can attend cross-national studies and the limitations that are inherent in them should be noted at the outset. The process of comparison tends to capture how we think; we describe one object based on its similarity to or difference from another. Looking at other political systems enables us not only to see our own in bolder relief but also to have yardsticks by which to measure qualities of various models. That France is a civil law system, in other words, has little real meaning except in contrast to the common law model or to other alternatives. The commonalities, as well as the variations, are highlighted when we compare. The allure of the comparative method has not translated into a large body of comparative judicial research. Much of what has been published about foreign legal/judicial politics focuses on a single country, and little is provided explicitly in the way of contrasts among national courts. A number of collections have been offered in which a common topic is treated more or less from the same perspective by a number of authors,[95] but the country-by-country format is perpetuated.

A number of explanations have been suggested for the lack of comparative work in the area of judicial politics. One is that legal questions do not travel well;[96] that observation most likely stems from the misguided belief that court functions are so "system specific" that the level of generalization possible is minimized.[97] I doubt that courts are any more bound by peculiar specificities than are legislatures, executives, or political parties. Courts perform basically the same functions of conflict resolution, social control, and, to varying degrees, policy-making in most societies. Another argument is the difficulty of mastering two languages—the language of the country and the language of law. That requirement admittedly presents an obstacle, but it can be overcome. A more likely valid explanation is the absence of "explicit macro-theoretical frameworks."[98] There is no taxonomy for classification or measurement across national boundaries. The result is that much of what purports to be comparative judicial research is descriptive or draws on such a variety of jurisprudential or political theories that comparability is lost.

The comparative method, even when applied to other political spheres, is plagued with problems of both theory and method. Sartori hit on part of the problem that remains acutely relevant for cross-national legal studies: the need for clear conceptualization that can be followed by empirical investigation. Data can be gathered only when the use of that information is clear.[99] Then higher levels of classification and abstraction and greater generalization are possible. Discriminating categories are essential as "statistical, computerized sophistication is no remedy for misinformation."[100]

Lijphart also tried to delineate the path that separates the comparative method from others, e.g., experimental or statistical, by explaining that comparison is a method, not a technique; its aim is "establishing general empirical propositions." But the problem lies in too many variables combined with a small number of cases.[101] He later revisited that difficulty and recommended methods for overcoming it: "(1) increasing the number of cases as much as possible by extending the analysis both geographically and historically; (2) reducing the property-space of the analysis by combining variables and/or categories; (3) focusing the analysis on comparable cases (i.e., cases that are similar in a large number of important characteristics, but dissimilar with regard to the variables between which a relationship is hypothesized) . . . and (4) restricting the analysis to the key variables and omitting those of only marginal importance."[102] The comparable case strategy, he concluded, was the most fruitful one if "the cases are selected in such a way as to maximize the variance of the independent variables and to minimize the variance of the control variables."[103]

The execution of comparative political research must meet standards of reliability and validity, or equivalence, levels of analysis, and predictability.[104] The application of the comparative method to legal/judicial politics seems to multiply those demands. Even in domestic political-judicial research, a number of common problems have been noted. One is the failure to conceive independent variables explicitly; another is the related difficulty in defining "as fully as possible the dependent variables, the set of 'meaningful acts,' " such as judicial decisions, they claim to help explain.[105] Researchers have been urged to consider the origins of the judicial phenomena they examine, particularly in light of controversial political choices made historically. Finally, public law scholars focusing on institutional relations sometimes fail to question how earlier political choices have influenced the institutions, whether intentionally or not.[106]

I have chosen to couch this study in democratic theory, though recognizing that such a vast literature says little about judicial power or judicial accountability. That body of thought does, nonetheless, suggest that all who exercise political power in democratic systems do so temporarily and conditionally. Conditionality is most apparently achieved where judges serve for fixed terms and must face the electorate. There are, however, other qualifications that apply and that render the judicial office somewhat temporary, even where tenure is granted for life. Notably, just as there are situations besides electoral defeat that dissuade elected officeholders from remaining, there are also circumstances whereby judges relinquish their offices without being formally removed. Possibilities short of removal can alter the behavior of other political elites, and the same holds for judicial officials. The dependent variable, judicial accountability, then is indicated by the judges who are removed, voluntarily resign or retire, or are otherwise sanctioned for failure to perform their duties objectively and impartially, free from corrupt or overtly partisan influences.

I follow also the comparable case strategy advocated by Lijphart. France, Italy, Britain, and the United States are all Western industrial or postindustrial nations; culturally and politically they are "geographically" related. Moreover, all four symbolically claim deference in their political structures to the rule of law and to the democratic rules of the game. These nations seem, therefore, to meet the criteria of similar cases, or at least their differences are within the realm of the "reasonably acceptable."[107] Because the historical evolution of the mechanisms for achieving judicial accountability in each will be considered, there is also a diachronic comparison within each country.[108]

The crucial differences we are seeking lie in the divergent methods that have been used both historically and contemporaneously for monitoring judicial accountability. Those variations stem from a number of potential independent variables that include legal culture (common law versus civil law traditions), judicial status (recruitment mechanisms), political environment, and judicial authority. The Guarnieri typology based on the autonomy and creativity of the judicial office will be used in the concept of judicial authority. These factors, I hypothesize, combine to mold the system each nation has adopted for monitoring judicial behavior and the ethical norms that define acceptable judicial conduct. The taxonomy of forms of judicial responsibility synthesized by Cappelletti (political accountability to other branches of government, societal or public accountability, vicarious state accountability, and personal legal accountability) will serve to classify monitoring mechanisms. The relationships that are explored are illustrated in figure 1, and I anticipate that the findings, while hardly predictive, will aid in explaining the phenomenon of judicial accountability. They will constitute a first step in the exploration of the dilemma that judicial authority poses in democracies.

Actions of courts and judges may enhance or diminish regime legitimacy. Legitimacy is often described, perhaps uncritically, in the context of law and justice. Though legitimacy remains an amorphous term, the measurement of which seems to have eluded scholarly agreement, it seems to entail "the capacity of the system to engender and maintain the belief that the existing political institutions are the most appropriate ones for the society"; its connotation "is evaluative."[109] It is, in other words, a moral concept in the sense that "a government is legitimate if what it does is right

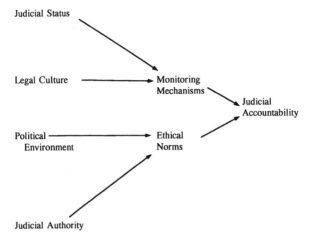

Figure 1. Model of Judicial Accountability

both in the sense of complying with certain fundamental principles, and . . . of being in line with prevailing cultural values."[110] Some of the basic functions of government, such as external defense, may be outside the scope of judicial interpretation, but providing for security or maintaining law and order usually contains a judicial element. The perceived legitimacy of the judiciary molds and at the same time reflects citizen beliefs about government as a whole. Parliaments and executives derive their legitimacy from the electorate, but judges "have a hand in law-making . . . without the sanction of universal suffrage."

Chapter 2

France

Jacqueline Lucienne Lafon

France has not only a long national heritage but also the most widely imitated judicial system in the world. "The popularity and acceptance of the French judicial system among the older as well as the newer states of the world represent," according to Abraham, "approval in the highest degree."[1] The historical evolution of the French systems for selecting and removing judges offers three distinct models. Under the Ancien Régime judges obtained their offices through venality and consequently owned their positions; during the Revolution of 1789 they were elected; now they are appointed by the executive, as they have been since the constitution of *frimaire* 22, eighth year of the Republic (December 13, 1799). The current system was inspired primarily by Napoleon Bonaparte.[2] Each of these practices reflects a particular historical era and a corresponding national mentality.

Exemplary behavior has historically been expected of judges in France and elsewhere. Still, the first principles of a disciplinary regime were not instituted until the nineteenth century. They are the early foundation of the system that was established under the Fifth Republic in the statutory ordinance of December 22, 1958. In a public charge of May 1832, André Marie Dupin, the celebrated head of the prosecution (*procureur général*) attached to the Cour de cassation, stated the primary principle behind any disciplinary system: "l'inamovibilité ne veut pas dire impunité: . . . cela ne le soustrait ni à l'empire des lois générales, ni au jugement de la magistrature elle-mê me" (irremovability does not mean impunity: . . . it does not put him [the judge] above the law nor does it insulate him from the judgment of the magistrature itself).[3]

The ideology of the French Revolution represented the antithesis of a disciplinary system for judges.[4] Judges were elected and were, therefore, regarded as an emanation of the nation. They were expected to be above all suspicion, and if they failed during their terms (two years for justices of the peace, four years for judges *en cassation,* and six years for both district judges and *accusateurs publics*), they had little chance of reelection. The electorate was their judge. This interpretation is not merely theoretical but is confirmed by historical facts. In July 1792, Minister of Justice Joly denounced the unprofessional attitudes of some judges. He claimed that some justices of the peace were not punctual or rigorous and that assistant judges did not always appear when they were required. No official sanction followed. Only a hostile attitude toward the regime, pretended or real, could have raised suspicion, and the negligent judges had failings that could not be considered of a political character. Also, the revolution had not yet become drastic; the Tribunal révolutionnaire, which was competent to try traitors and which generally imposed death sentences, was created later, on March 9, 1793.

The Ancien Régime and the more recent period of the nineteenth and twentieth centuries are eras rich in contrasts. The two periods stand in total opposition to one another: in the former the judge owned his office; in the latter he was dependent on executive power, and that dependency evolved into a civil service regiment. The body that was competent to hear complaints was different in each system, as were the punishments available. There has been, nonetheless, a persistent conception that a judge's comportment must be above reproach. Over time that concept developed into a system.

Studying the accountability of judges and the discipline of errant ones is difficult; the topic has not been approached in conjunction with the Ancien Régime or, for that matter, with the nineteenth and twentieth centuries. The archives of these eras, through World War II, have never been fully researched, but from what has been written, some examples of ethical misconduct can be gleaned and some conclusions drawn. The difficulty is greater for the more recent period. The Archives of the Fourth Republic (1946–58) are hard to locate. The practice under the Fifth Republic is no easier to consider, but for different reasons. The Ministry of Justice (Chancellerie) in Paris maintains the records of all proceedings, but they are, as elsewhere, confidential. Fortunately, the former undersecretary of the magistrature (sous directeur de la Magistrature), Bernard Darcos, was extremely cooperative and provided current information through the summer of 1991, without violating confidentiality, about specific disciplinary proceedings, offenses, and sanctions. These data have not been published or analyzed previously.

The Ancien Régime

In a speech given twice a year (the Mercuriales), the first president of courts of parliament or the head of the Prosecution Department would proclaim the virtues that a magistrate should possess under the Ancien Régime. They would portray an ideal figure even though they were fully aware that they were addressing mere mortals. In this fashion, they intended to remind both judges and prosecutors of their proper roles. They largely succeeded, but there were always exceptions. The cases of misconduct that are reported in monographs are scarce and must be treated cautiously. They focus solely on the jurisdiction before which the case was brought, the offenses alleged, and the sanctions imposed.[5]

Upon an allegation of misconduct, the chief of the court would open an investigation. If he was the one accused, however, the chief of the next higher jurisdiction would take charge. This practice is revealed by the proceedings in the 1665 Tardieu case, in which the magistrate responsible for criminal cases (*lieutenant criminel*) of the Châtelet de Paris was accused of corruption. The first president of the Parliament of Paris, the superior jurisdiction, initiated the inquiry. The accused magistrate was judged by his peers unless he had a male relative sitting in that jurisdiction. In that case he would ask that the case be heard in another jurisdiction of equal importance. This procedure was used in 1608 when Beaulieu, a counselor in the Parliament of Bordeaux, disclaimed jurisdiction for the court, and the case was heard instead by the Parliament of Rennes.

Royal jurisdictions were apparently jealous of their disciplinary prerogatives, as in the following example of how jurisdictional competence was determined. In 1496, Claude de Chauvreux, a cleric and counselor in the Parliament of Paris, was accused of forging a proxy (*procuration*). Fearing that he might invoke his clerical privilege to be tried by an ecclesiastical jurisdiction, the parliament declared that Chauvreux had forfeited his ecclesiastical status and proceeded to judge him.

Magistrates could be disciplined for two kinds of conduct: offenses against professional standards and offenses in private life. Violations of professional ethics are documented as early as the fourteenth century, and the punishments inflicted were harsh. A counselor in the Parliament of Paris in 1348 was convicted of altering witnesses' statements; he was condemned to be strangled and hanged. The previously mentioned cleric Chauvreux, found guilty in 1496, was likewise punished severely, being stripped of his office, subjected to *exauctoration,* and banished eternally from the kingdom. Exauctoration, a painful and humiliating public ritual that has been traced to the fifteenth century, was the reverse of formally investing a magistrate. A judge condemned to a painful or degrading punishment or even to death wore his official red robe for the last time. He would be brought before his peers and forced to kneel while carrying a torch as the sentence was read. Then the court ushers would seize his judge's robe and insignia and replace them with a garment and bonnet of rough serge. The executioner would lead the condemned to a public place and brand him on the forehead with the fleur de lys. The public and exemplary nature of the punishment constituted one of the main notions of deterrence during the Ancien Régime.

Exauctoration was rarely imposed as the only punishment but was rather used in conjunction with others. A president of the Parliament of Toulouse in 1536, found guilty of accepting a bribe, was subjected not only to exauctoration but also to life imprisonment in the Castle of St. Malo. A counselor of the Parliament of Normandy, convicted in 1540 of embezzlement and abuse, was subjected to the exauctoration ritual, curiously without the brand of the fleur de lys; all of his property was confiscated and he was banished from the kingdom for life. Seventeen years later, however, he was reinstated to his office by the king despite the parliament's yearlong protest.

Extortion was punished by exauctoration in 1437, but in 1528 a counselor of the Parliament of Toulouse who was found guilty of revealing secrets of the court and committing unscrupulous behavior was only deprived of his office. Such inconsistencies are further demonstrated by the 1585 case of a counselor in the Parliament of Bordeaux who was found to be unscrupulous, fined heavily, and deprived of his office. He was, however, reinstated after the king rescinded the decision. The parliament was forced to accept him but imposed the restrictions that he was only to preside and was to sign judgments as infrequently as possible. Even these limitations were revoked by the king in 1594. This kind of monarchal interference was observable during this period not only in France but, as will be seen later, in England as well.

Judges could be punished not only for professional misconduct, but also for offenses committed in their private lives, from trivial to serious. In 1640 Broca, a counselor in the Parliament of Pau, with the help of one of his valets, beat a magistrate serving on the court with him. His case went before the Parliament of Toulouse, which declared him unworthy of exercising any position in the judiciary. A counselor from Toulouse involved in a coinage offense case was exonerated in 1713 but was forbidden to act as a counselor. The advantage to the counselor of this type of condemnation was that, as owner of his office, he could still sell or rent it. Rental was a means of retaining the office until a son was old enough to assume the position. Though these affairs concerned strictly private behavior, they were nonetheless sanctioned by specific disciplinary measures, not through ordinary punishment.

There were even cases of discipline involving magistrates who had committed murder. If the magistrate was not excused because of some mitigating circumstance, he received two sentences: the common criminal punishment and a sentence specific to the judicial position. A counselor in the Parliament of Bordeaux was tried in 1570 for the murder of his wife and her lover. He had killed them when he discovered them in his home, and the following day he presented himself to the court. Even though convicted, he received royal letters of forgiveness and remission, presumably because he had committed a crime of passion. In 1600, Beaulieu, the counselor in the Parliament of Bordeaux mentioned earlier, strangled his wife. His motive was not clear, but his immediate flight seemed to confirm his guilt. He was tried in absentia and in 1602 was condemned to exauctoration and to having his fists and his head cut off. The sentence was executed in effigy as an example, since he was nowhere to be found. A *président à mortier* in the Parliament of Bourgogne killed his first cousin and a valet in 1638; his motive may have been that he had previously courted the wife of the murdered cousin. On May 8, 1643, the Parliament of Bourgogne sentenced him to death after having subjected him to a form of exauctoration.

Each of these latter cases demonstrates the double penalty, but it was not practiced consistently. For example, in 1611 a number of young men, including a counselor in the Parliament of Bordeaux, killed a nobleman who had eloped with an adolescent of good birth. The counselor's punishment was solely that of the common criminal—being condemned to death and executed in effigy. Similarly in 1784 a président à mortier of the Parliament of Provence murdered his wife and then disappeared. He, too, received a death sentence by default. These examples suggest that there must have been no general rule. Judicial crimes were treated according to the inclination of the judges, illustrative of the discretionary power (*pouvoir arbitraire*) that was so criticized at the end of the Ancien Régime.

In these cases of judicial discipline under the Ancien Régime, none, notably, involved political opinions. Eventually magistrates in courts of parliament criticized reforms made by the king but not the monarchy as a form of government. This attitude was to change considerably in the nineteenth century.

The Nineteenth and Twentieth Centuries

When Napoleon Bonaparte reorganized the judiciary, he also established the basis for a disciplinary regime. Thereafter one could refer to official texts when a decision was to be taken in individual cases, a significant innovation over the customary practices of the Ancien Régime. Political regimes rose and fell in rapid succession from the collapse of the First Empire in 1815 until the establishment of the Third Republic in 1875. This instability was accompanied by constitutional changes, but none altered the disciplinary system of the judges. Indeed, no major modifications were made until the constitution of the Fourth Republic on October 27, 1946. To understand this unsettled era, laws and practices must both be considered.

The Napoleonic system for disciplining judges was constructed over a period of 10 years, beginning with an elementary scheme in the laws of 1800 and 1802. By 1810 a complex procedure was completely in place, and its endurance throughout the nineteenth century testifies to its effectiveness. The law of August 30, 1883, and the decrees of 1934, 1935, and 1936 provided the final elements, but they were eventually modified by the constitution of October 27, 1946. These legal texts define the competent authorities, procedures, and sanctions. The notion of disciplinary fault, though, evolved considerably through the years in accordance with circumstances and events.

The constant principle of the laws from 1800 to 1936 is that judges should be disciplined within the corporation of judges. Whether by design or not, this principle is reminiscent of the Ancien Régime. Disciplinary procedures were refined over time, and the list of possible punishments was extended. The law of *ventôse* 27, eighth year of the Republic (March 18, 1800), affirmed the competence of the *section des requêtes* of the Tribunal de cassation, later called the Cour de cassation, to hear all allegations of judicial misbehavior. It examined the requests forwarded to the Cour de cassation for verification of legality. The law provided for two separate proceedings, depending on the circumstances. The public prosecutor could charge magistrates with what might be considered professional faults: exceeding one's power (*excès de pouvoir*) or offenses committed in the discharge of duties (article 80). If, in the course of a procedure for annulment before the Cour de cassation, the civil or criminal section uncovered actions involving forfeiture or faults in judicial actions, the alternative procedure allowed the facts to be submitted to the section des requêtes. That section then acted as a jury of accusation (article 82). The judge could be tried by a criminal jurisdiction and, if he appealed to the Tribunal de cassation, the section that had originally made the allegations could not again be involved.

The magistrature in France, as in most of continental Europe, has two branches, the bench and the prosecution. The first law governing judicial conduct that clearly distinguished the procedures appropriate for each branch was the *senatus-consulte* of *thermidor* 16, tenth year of the Republic (August 4, 1802). That law instituted the office of Grand Juge, or minister of justice (article 78). His authority extended to all jurisdictions of the magistrature (article 81), and he presided over the Tribunal de cassation in its larger context, not just over the section des requêtes when it reviewed judicial misconduct of magistrates of the bench belonging to the appeals courts and criminal tribunals (article 82). Allegations had to be serious (*cause grave*), and the sanction imposed was suspension. The Tribunal de cassation could eventually demand that any accused judge explain his conduct to the Grand Juge (article 82). The head of the Prosecution Department of the Tribunal de cassation supervised the prosecutors of the courts of appeal; they themselves supervised the prosecutors in the lower courts, the *tribunaux civils* (article 84).

The law of April 20, 1810, further elaborated on the judicial discipline system and was particularly complex in the procedures applying to judges of the bench. This law introduced a preliminary phase in which the presidents of the courts or tribunals were able to warn ex officio or on demand of the public prosecutor when a judge compromised the dignity of the office (article 49, *dignité de leur caractère*). If a warning (*avertissement*) was insufficient, the judge could be formally punished in one of the following ways: censure, censure with reprimand (in which case salary was suspended for one month), or temporary suspension with no salary for the period of suspension (article 50). An accused judge was also given a number of guarantees. No decision could be made until the judge had been heard and the prosecutor had announced his conclusions (article 55). Decisions by lower courts were reviewed by the imperial court of the resort (article

51), and the imperial court could commence an action if the appropriate lower court neglected to do so (article 54). The decision of the imperial court was forwarded to the Grand Juge and, when involving a penalty of censure with reprimand or temporary suspension, was subject to the minister's approval before taking effect (article 56). In the case of a temporary suspension, on the other hand, the judge automatically stopped exercising his duties until a final decision was announced by the Grand Juge. The Grand Juge could, if the charges were very serious, refer the case to the Cour de cassation under provisions of article 82 of the law of 1802 (article 56).

An innovation in the law of 1810 concerned judges found guilty of even the most minor crime. If a convicted judge was assumed to have been involved in some reprehensible act in his private life, the record of the case was to be forwarded to the Grand Juge. The minister could then determine whether to begin disciplinary procedures in the Cour de cassation, which could result in withdrawal of the judge's rights (*déchéance*) or suspension (article 59).

Members of the Prosecution Department were likewise liable. If they were guilty of reprehensible conduct (*conduite répréhensible*), they would be reminded of their duties by the head of the Prosecution Department in their territorial jurisdiction, and the Grand Juge was informed (article 60). Moreover, the imperial courts and the *cours d'assises* were also to notify the Grand Juge if members of the prosecution did not live up to the obligations of their position or compromised their honor, honesty, and dignity (*s'écartent du devoir de leur état et compromettent l'honneur, la délicatesse et la dignité*). Lower courts were to inform the first president and the head of the prosecution of the imperial court (article 61).

Whichever procedure applied, the minister of justice held the ultimate decision. He could summon the accused magistrates from either the bench or the prosecution and ask them to explain their conduct (articles 57 and 60).

The law of August 30, 1883, can be viewed as completing the disciplinary regime that originated at the beginning of the century, for two reasons. First, it institutionalized the Cour de cassation, all sections assembled, as the disciplinary body and named it the Conseil Supérieur de la Magistrature (Superior Council of Magistrature, or CSM). This body was authorized to discipline judges of the bench (articles 13 and 14) when cases were brought before it by the minister of justice, at that time called the Garde des Sceaux. Hence, the CSM was empowered to impose punishments after hearing the case (article 16). The possible sanctions were not specified in the law, and commentators concluded that the options were, therefore, the same as those cited in the law of 1810 and in the decree of March 1, 1852, article 4, which had introduced forfeiture or withdrawal of rights. Though there was no mention of a warning, commentators decided that this possibility was also retained from the earlier law. The minister of justice supervised all judges of both the bench and prosecution and could reprimand them if necessary (article 17). A reprimand, however, was not synonymous with punishment, at least according to those analyzing the law. The minister could also, as before, summon a magistrate for an explanation of questionable actions (article 17). The second important point in the law of 1883 was the extended definition of disciplinary fault.

There was no change in the law concerning members of the Prosecution Department until the twentieth century. They were obliged to comply with all instructions given hierarchically and were not protected by the guarantee of nonremovability. On June 5, 1934, Minister of Justice Henry Chéron proposed a decree establishing the rules in cases of revocation, retrogradation, or mandatory transfer. The decree granted essential guarantees to prosecutors without infringing on the prerogatives of the government. The president of the republic signed the decree the same day. Also, a consultative commission was created that automatically included the head of prosecution of the Cour de cassation (who presided), the two senior magistrates of the bench on that court, and the senior director at the Ministry of Justice. Two other members were appointed by the minister of justice: the head of prosecution of a court of appeal and one representative of the Prosecution Department of the lower jurisdictions. Another person was elected from among all members of the Prosecution Department of the rank equal to that of the accused judge. The accused was guaranteed the right to be heard and to present a defense. After hearing the accused judge, the consultative commission gave advice to the minister of justice. If one of the three sanctions was to be imposed, it was announced in a decree.

A decree of January 10, 1935, brought minute additional changes. It provided that the president of the commission acting alone, instead of the commission as a whole, would designate the judge in charge of an inquiry. Another decree, of October 31, 1936, maintained the earlier rules but applied them only in cases of potential revocation.

This system for policing the actions of magistrates, begun by Napoleon Bonaparte and completed by the law of 1883 and the decrees of 1934, 1935, and 1936, lasted 146 years, until the constitution of the Fourth Republic, October 27, 1946. The Fourth Republic broke with the earlier practices for the bench by transferring the disciplinary prerogative from the Cour de cassation to an institution that was new except for its name, Conseil Supérieur de la Magistrature (article 84). The new CSM was composed of fourteen members, including the president of the republic and the minister of justice. Six notables and their substitutes, who could not be deputies, were elected by a two-thirds majority of the National Assembly. Four, along with substitutes, were named from among the judges according to their ranks, and the method of their election was specified by the law of February 1, 1947. The last two members and their substitutes were chosen by the president of the republic from those who had judicial functions but were in neither the judiciary nor Parliament. In 1947, both of the last two were lawyers, as was one substitute, but the other substitute's profession was not specified. In 1953, the same two lawyers were reappointed, as was the substitute who was also a lawyer, but the other substitute was a member of the Council of State (Conseil d'Etat). All except the two politicians served six-year terms. This version of the Conseil Supérieur de la Magistrature was criticized primarily because the number of judges required by the law as members was relatively small. But the practice more or less counterbalanced the theory. In 1947 the members of the council were eleven judges, five lawyers, two law professors and one former minister; in 1953, nine judges, three lawyers, one councillor of state, and the remaining professions undetermined. In any case, the judges represented at least half of the members. Another cause of alarm was the fear of political influence relating to the roles of the president and vice-president of the CSM. Though they did not participate when the disciplinary section of the commission studied the case (the CSM was divided into three sections), they did attend the plenary sessions when decisions were made. These criticisms may have affected subsequent reforms made in the constitution of 1958.

The CSM of 1946 had jurisdiction only over judges of the bench, as had been the case with the earlier council, but its functions were wider. The new CSM was to ensure judges' independence and to administer the courts. The constitution of 1946 and the laws of February 1 and March 11, 1947, did not mention either procedure or range of punishments. The result was, again, referral to the texts of the nineteenth century.

The new constitution and implementing legislation made no reference to the discipline of members of the Prosecution Department, as there had been a major change in treatment of allegations of misbehavior among prosecuting magistrates in the decree of June 5, 1934, as modified by decrees of January 10, 1935, and October 31, 1936.

The laws that defined the disciplinary organ and its procedures, powers, and sanctions also dealt with the notion of disciplinary fault. The law of March 18, 1800, alluded to the professional faults of actions exceeding a judge's power, technical offenses in performance of duties (article 80), and forfeiture (article 82). The Law of August 4, 1802, added cause grave, or serious cause (article 82). The law of April 20, 1810, was more specific. It clearly defined one fault relevant to judges both of the bench and of the prosecution—being absent without leave. A judge who was guilty of this transgression was deprived of his salary. If he remained absent for more than six months, he could be treated as having resigned. Even one month's absence could result in termination. The head of prosecution could order the judge to return to his post after a month, and if that order were not obeyed, the absence was reported to the Grand Juge. The absent judge was at that time considered to have resigned, and the Grand Juge could propose a replacement to the emperor (article 48).

The law of 1810 also enumerated a number of "reprehensible attitudes" or actions. Article 49 condemned the judge of the bench who imperiled the dignity of his office, and article 60 prohibited reprehensible conduct for officers of the Prosecution Department. Article 61 defined the duties of such a judgeship (*devoir de son état*) and condemned actions "compromising the honor, scrupulousness or dignity of the office." Curiously, the general terms describing improper behavior varied according to the category of judgeship, and though they all undoubtedly referred primarily to judges' actions in the course of their official duties, they might also apply to activities in private life if the conduct was notorious. But what, exactly, was "reprehensible conduct"? The vague terminology was susceptible to exploitation by the political powers.

France experienced six political regimes during the nineteenth century, and because judges were named by the executive, they were responsive to the expectations of the government. Indeed, at each change of regime, the executive managed to obtain control of the magistrature through purges, using direct or indirect means.[6] Some judges who were retained might nonetheless express hostile attitudes toward the government. In such cases, one of the vague disciplinary faults in the laws of 1802 and 1810 could easily be applied to the judge's political attitudes.

This theme was developed in the Fouquet case in 1832 by Dupin, the head of prosecution in the Cour de cassation.[7] Fouquet was a judge in the tribunal de la Seine, who had given his approval for publication of an article under his name in a Legitimist newspaper, *La Gazette de France*. The article opposed the reigning King Louis-Philippe and sided with Legitimists faithful to the direct heir of Charles X. Fouquet was charged before the Cour de cassation, where Dupin accused him of compromising the dignity of his office. Dupin acknowledged that there should be a distinction between being a citizen and being a judge but argued that judges must respect the "obligation of reserve." Fouquet was found guilty of compromising the dignity of his judgeship and of committing a serious fault; he was censured and reprimanded.

Dupin's accusation in 1832 is famous because it originated the concept "obligation of reserve," an intentionally ambiguous expression adopted in the ordinance of 1958, to the widest field of magistrates' activities. He developed his theory further over the years, according to the proposition that civil servants could not separate their public roles from their private lives. Those in public office were always in their public character and thereby relinquished some of the liberty that an ordinary citizen might enjoy.

The notion of political reserve was finally made official in the law of August 30, 1883, article 14: "All political deliberation is forbidden to the judiciary. All hostile manifestations or demonstrations to the principle or to the form of government of the Republic is forbidden to judges. The violation of these dispositions constitutes a disciplinary fault."

The general concept of fault was enlarged considerably after 1810 but might not have extended professional culpability to include political attitudes had the nineteenth century not been so politically unstable. The limitations on judges' political leanings were not, however, the only restrictions placed on magistrates' behavior. According to the cases that are recorded, disciplinary actions against magistrates were pursued also for political attitudes, transgressions of professional standards, and notorious private misconduct.[8]

From the perspective of violating professional standards, judges in the nineteenth and twentieth centuries were not very different from those of the Ancien Régime. During the more recent period, as in the former, some were found to be unscrupulous (*indélicat*). One judge in 1806, for example, was twice accused of dishonesty; he resigned after the second allegation. Almost a century later, in 1903, a magistrate in the Court of Appeal of Paris was implicated in a financial affair; he ceased his activities and was forced into retirement. The option of a simple retirement is starkly different, however, from the punishments meted out under the Ancien Régime; its moderate severity is a modern phenomenon. It was consistent with the civil service statute developed in the nineteenth century, whereby the age of retirement was fixed in a decree of March 1, 1852, and the principle of a pension was affirmed in the law of June 9, 1853.

Moderation is seen also in other cases. In 1876 a judge was found guilty of having cheated in games; that was a private action but publicly known. He was also found to have accepted several valuables in exchange for his intervention in annulling a sale. The judge was merely censured for professional faults. Falsifying documents was another classic violation of ethics. A magistrate in 1844 in the Court of Appeal in Grenoble had altered the date on a promissory note that was part of a civil procedure. When criminal proceedings against him were contemplated, he resigned.

In addition to the preceding examples of professional misbehavior, which had been recognized during the Ancien Régime, in the nineteenth century a new professional fault was introduced: insubordination on the part of the prosecution for political reasons. The procureur général of the Court of Appeal in Paris refused to prosecute General Boulanger in 1889 for allegedly imperiling the institutions of the Third Republic in 1888, after he retired from the army. The procureur général was removed from office for insubordination.

Judges were also liable for any notorious private conduct, and women and gambling led more than one of them astray. Judges who disgraced their families or family life in general were subject to disciplinary sanctions. In a typical case, a judge was brought before the Tribunal de cassation on *germinal* 2, eighth year of the Republic (March 23, 1800), for openly and publicly living with a woman to whom he was not married, in the same town where he was serving. He even claimed their children as legitimate at the registry office in charge of civil status, when they were the issue of an adulterous liaison. Similarly, in 1863 a judge who was married and had children was punished for maintaining his mistress in the family home. In 1885 a president of a court was disciplined for receiving women of ill-repute in his office for his personal convenience. The punishments for such private misbehavior could be harsh. A magistrate in the Court of Appeal in Toulouse was found in a brothel in 1843 and consequently invited to resign. Another was removed from office in 1882 for scandalous immorality.

Gambling could be equally as perilous as licentiousness for a judge. In 1875 the *avocat général*, or public prosecutor, assigned to the Court of Appeal in Paris lost so much money at gambling that he became financially destitute, and for that he was removed from his position.

During the Monarchy of July (1830–48), several Legitimist and Republican judges were punished for falling short of expectations under Dupin's theory of the obligation of reserve. The practice waned in the second half of the nineteenth century, only to reemerge in the Third Republic. A judge in 1879 assisted in a banquet organized in opposition to the constitution of the Third Republic and, at the conclusion of the event, proposed the toast "Long live the King." That incident, reported to the Cour de cassation, resulted in his removal from office.

The president of the tribunal civil in Orange went into the court of justice on July 14, 1881 (Bastille Day) and ordered the removal of the candles forming the letters *R.F.* (République française), which had been installed for the national holiday, and he even broke some of the candles with his cane. The Cour de cassation concluded that he had not respected the obligation of reserve and suspended him for one month. This case is the origin of the law of 1883, already mentioned. Hereafter, there was no difficulty in punishing a judge who openly expressed a hostile political attitude. Within three months, 614 judges were removed,[9] but afterwards the law was applied according to the circumstances of the case. An assistant judge in the tribunal of first instance in Riom in 1888 used the pretext of distributing prizes at a congregational school to attack the government by denouncing the anticlerical laws on education. The Conseil Supérieur de la Magistrature censured him.

As this historical summary suggests, the notion of disciplinary fault evolved through both jurisprudence and law. Professional faults, unscrupulous actions, and notorious private misbehavior are all continuous themes from the Ancien Régime until the twentieth century. The major innovation of the nineteenth century was the introduction of the obligation of reserve, with its political implications. As for the punishments that could be applied to an erring judge, there was a substantial divergence from one period to the next that corresponded to the larger societal context. The Ancien Régime used sanctions intended to repress behavior through severe public punishment, whereas in the nineteenth century judicial behavior was subject to the new civil service statute. To what extent did this pattern of development continue into the Fifth Republic?

The Disciplinary Regime under the Fifth Republic

A local riot in Algiers on May 13, 1958, demonstrated the weakness and inefficacy of the authorities of the Fourth Republic and signaled its disintegration. A new constitution, that of October 4, 1958, instituted the Fifth Republic. That constitution organized the powers of government and in title

8 defined the judicial authority. The constitution created a new CSM composed of nine members and prescribed that the rules concerning appointments to it would be fixed by a statutory ordinance. It also affirmed the disciplinary function of the CSM for judges of the bench (articles 64 and 65), but these principles required further development.

Two ordinances providing specifics followed shortly, on December 22, 1958, one on the statute of the magistrature and the other on the CSM. The statutory ordinance concerning the magistrates also addressed the disciplinary regime. Whether intentionally or not, the overall concept of discipline was an obvious reflection of centuries of evolution and development, even if some particulars were not precisely the same. The terms of the ordinance elaborating the composition of the CSM were, on the other hand, apparently a reaction against the institution created in 1946. These two texts were applied for more than three decades, time enough to draw conclusions about the attendant practices. In time, they too were criticized. The statutory ordinance was modified by two organic laws, the first of February 25, 1992, and the second of February 5, 1994. The CSM was completely changed by an organic law, also dated February 5, 1994, followed by an application decree and decision, both on March 9, 1994. Only in a few years' time can the implications of the new CSM be evaluated, but a theoretical consideration of the reform provides an interesting comparison of the laws.

The statutory ordinance of December 22, 1958, specified the rules of behavior that a judge must respect. Failure to comply with that code of conduct would bring a judge into disciplinary proceedings and result in his punishment. Article 43 defined disciplinary fault: "All breaches committed by a judge in the discharge of his function, against honor, scrupulousness or dignity, constitute a disciplinary fault." This sweeping definition raises a number of issues. The expressions used in 1958 are replicas of those mentioned in the law of April 20, 1810, article 61, concerning the duties of judges belonging to the prosecution ("devoirs de son état . . . , honneur, délicatesse, dignité"). The legislature of 1958 applied that definition indiscriminately to judges of the bench and those of the prosecution, because the domain was wider and hence more vague. The more ambiguous the terminology, the more convenient for a government and the more precarious for a judge. (The ordinance of 1958, however, also provides for guarantees to judges to avoid such abuses.) Interpretations of the language become, as a result, all-important.

A term such as "scrupulousness" is relatively easy to understand, but to fail in one's "honor or dignity" is susceptible to a number of possible interpretations. The latter phrase is potentially applicable to both professional and private actions, at least if private undertakings are notorious. The more precise 1810 text had specifically addressed "honor and dignity in the function." In the final analysis, only the first part of the definition "all breaches committed . . . in the discharge of his function" is doubtful. What constitutes "the discharge of his function"? The answer apparently lies in the obligations of a judge; this interpretation comports with actual practice. The obligations are enumerated in the preceding articles of the statutory ordinance. Article 5 requires hierarchical subordination of judges of the prosecution. This principle is mitigated by the old adage "My pen is servile, but my word is free." Article 6 mentions the oath of office and in doing so alludes to the obligation of secrecy and confidentiality of deliberations. Articles 8 and 9 affirm the incompatibility of holding multiple functions. Article 10 acknowledges the obligation of reserve, and it borrows in its first two phrases the definition contained in the law of 1883: "All political deliberation is forbidden to the judiciary." Finally, article 13 refers to the requirement of residence. Article 10 is important because it demonstrates that there is a continuity with the law of 1883. The statutory ordinance is, therefore, a complete synthesis of the texts of the nineteenth century that defined disciplinary faults, and should such a fault be found, a judge is subject to discipline.

A judge who is faced with a disciplinary proceeding is marked, his or her career compromised. For that reason, preliminary measures were organized to avoid recourse to formal proceedings. The preliminary procedure requires that the first president of a Court of Appeal or the head of the Prosecution Department assigned to that court be informed that a subordinate judge is not meeting the expectations of the office. There is then a choice of punishing the judge with a negative evaluation. In fact, the chief of a court rates all subordinate judges after receiving advice from the president of the tribunal de grande instance. Since the reform of 1992, the evaluation is given every two years, rather than annually. These evaluations influence promotions. A negative evaluation, in other words, can temporarily block a judge's advancement and presumably correct the offending behavior.

If the allegation is more serious, however, the first president of the Court of Appeal or the counterpart in the prosecution may give the erring judge a warning. This practice was introduced in the law of 1810, and though it is not an actual punishment, the warning is noted in the judge's file and its seriousness cannot be discounted. A law of amnesty allows for purging these annotations at some later time unless the charges involve dignity and honor. Several amnesties occurred in the last few years, which perhaps explain the reform of 1992. The warning is automatically obliterated after three years if no other warning has been made and no disciplinary sanction taken. The statutory ordinance of 1958 did not treat the warning as a disciplinary measure or punishment, but the Council of State in the 1972 Obrego decision declared that the implications of a warning are sufficiently serious to warrant providing the same guarantees to the accused judge as in a formal procedure.

The chief of court has the discretion to decide if the accusations can be resolved with a warning or if they are to be forwarded to the Chancellerie (Ministry of Justice). When allegations arrive at the ministry, an investigation is undertaken. If the charges are not overly grave, the undersecretary for the magistrature may summon the judge and negotiate a solution, such as a change of post. Should that avenue fail, then the formal procedure begins with either the report of the chief of court or the investigation report.

The minister of justice initiates the formal procedure. If the complaint or the facts alleged seem sufficiently serious, he can deem the case to be urgent. He then decides on the proposal of the judge's superiors to suspend the judge's functions until a decision is made whether to pursue the charges. The judge's salary is not affected during that period. If the accused judge was from the bench, such a measure formerly occurred after the CSM, which would hear the case, gave its advice. The reform of 1992 slightly modified this procedure. If the matter involves a judge of the bench, the minister of justice, on the recommendation of the judge's superiors, can propose to the CSM that the judge be forbidden to exercise official functions without depriving the judge of salary. In the case of a member of the prosecution, the minister of justice makes the decision on the recommendation of the magistrate's superiors, after advice from the Commission de Discipline du Parquet (CDP). Then if the minister does not approach the CSM or the CDP within two months to initiate the disciplinary procedure, the temporary suspension ceases automatically. The only change introduced by the organic law of 1994 is the replacement of the CDP by the competent section of the CSM for the Prosecution Department.

The name Conseil Supérieur de la Magistrature was resurrected for the second time to apply to a wholly new reality. The ordinance of December 22, 1958, concerning the CSM provided that the president of the republic preside over the council and the minister of justice serve as the vice president. This arrangement does not apply, however, when the CSM is acting as a disciplinary body. In that situation, the 1958 laws designated the first president of the Cour de cassation as the presiding officer for the group of nine members named by the president of the republic. They served for four-year terms that were renewable once. Three of the members were from the Cour de cassation, including an avocat général as a representative of the prosecution, and three others were judges of the bench from the lower jurisdictions. All six judges had to be chosen from a list submitted by a body designed to help the first president in the administration of the court, the Bureau de la Cour de cassation; its members were the first president, the two highest representatives of the prosecution, and the presidents of chambers. The seventh member of the CSM was a counselor of state selected from a list of three presented by the general assembly of the Council of State. The final two members were notables from outside the judiciary.

Through the years, the manner of selection of the nine members of the CSM drew criticism, and a reform was proposed in March 1991 by Minister of Justice Henri Nallet. Because the total number of representatives could not be altered without changing the constitution, the only possible changes were in the method of designating the members. The reform proposed reducing from six to four the number of judges selected under the old system. The remaining two would be a judge of a Court of Appeal and one from a tribunal de grande instance, who would be selected from a list of six names proposed by the Commission of Advancement, a group regarded as representative of the magistrature in its entirety.[10] Nonetheless, the CSM still appeared to be in the hands of the executive, a political power. Representatives of the judges' unions regarded the reform project as a *minimum minimorum* and both the left-wing Syndicat de la Magistrature and the right-wing Association Professionnelle des Magistrats protested with a *journée d'action* for May 16, 1991. In November of that year, President François Mitterrand announced that the constitution would be modified before the end of his term, in particular the article concerning the CSM. He had promised this when he was a candidate for the presidency the first time, in 1981.

On December 3, 1992, President Mitterrand, presiding over the Council of Ministers, appointed a committee to consider revision of the constitution and named the well-known jurist Dean Georges Vedel as its head. The committee presented its conclusions on February 15, 1993. As a result of the elections in March 1993, the majority in the National Assembly changed.

The newly constituted assembly took the Vedel committee's work and elaborated a new proposal on the CSM; this text was adopted by both chambers of Parliament and then by Parliament sitting in congress in Versailles on July 19, 1993.

In the revised version of article 65 of the constitution, the president of the republic still presides over the CSM, and the minister of justice acts as vice-president. The remainder of the article is more elaborate and perhaps more rational. The new CSM is divided into two sections of 10 members each. One section has authority over advancement and discipline of judges of the bench. It is composed of five judges of the bench and one officer of the prosecution. There is also one counselor of state designated by the Council of State and three notables who must not belong to Parliament or to the judiciary; one is appointed by the president of the republic, one by the president of the National Assembly, and one by the president of the Senate. The president of the Cour de cassation presides when this body hears a discipline case. The other section gives advice concerning the appointment of judges of the prosecution, except those designated in the Council of Ministers. It also advises in disciplinary cases and is then presided over by the head of the prosecution of the Cour de cassation. This half of the CSM is composed of five officers of the prosecution and one judge of the bench, the counselor of state, and the three notables from the other division.

The organic law of February 5, 1994, necessary to specify some practical elements, abrogates the 1958 ordinance on the CSM. The new CSM was implemented in June 1994. The law organizes the representation of the judges according to their classifications, and these representatives serve four-year terms that are not renewable immediately. The section that is competent for the bench includes one judge of the highest level in the Cour de cassation, who is elected by his or her peers; one first president of a Court of Appeal, elected by all of the first presidents at that level; one president of a tribunal de grande instance elected by the presidents of the tribunaux de grande instance and the presidents of the first instance jurisdictions (tribunaux de première instance). The two remaining judges of the bench and the judge of the prosecution are named through a two-degree election. This involves, for the judges of the bench except those enumerated above, an election of an assembly of 160 of their number, who then elect the remaining two judges to the CSM. The prosecution department elects an assembly of 80 that designates the last magistrate. The section that deals with judges of the prosecution has a parallel composition: one prosecutor from the highest level in the Cour de cassation, one public prosecutor from a Court of Appeal, and one prosecutor from a tribunal de grande instance, all elected by their peers. There are two additional prosecutors and one judge of the bench elected in the same two-degree election as their counterparts for the other section. A counselor of state is elected by the general assembly of the Council of State and may sit on either of the sections. The details of the electoral procedures and the deadline for holding elections were stated in a decree of March 9, 1994.

The extent to which the CSM has gained independence is difficult to measure. The presence of three members designated by the highest political notables raises some questions, but the provisions of the revised article 65 at least mark a clear break with past institutions in terms of the Prosecution Department. As will be seen shortly, the competent authority in disciplinary cases was formerly the minister of justice, who only took advice from the CDP. This commission is now void and has been replaced by the CSM. Though the CCP (Commission Consultative du Parquet) created in January 1992 to give advice on appointments to the Prosecution Department has not been officially annulled, it can be deduced from article 25 of the organic law of February 5, 1994, modifying a precedent disposition referring to this institution. The minister of justice has lost the privilege of choosing judges to sit on the disciplinary body but retains the power of final decision.

When the 1958 CSM took up a case, the accused judges had a number of legal guarantees that undoubtedly exceeded those available in 1810. They have been maintained with the new regulation of the CSM for all judges. The judge has the right to copies of the charges, his or her record, and all documents from the preliminary investigation. The procedure before the CSM is not public, but the judge has the right to be assisted by a lawyer or by a colleague and to demand the testimony of witnesses. Even a completely new investigation can eventually result.

Identical guarantees were already available to judges of the prosecution when they were tried in front of the Commission de Discipline du Parquet. This commission, created by article 59 of the 1958 statutory ordinance, was reminiscent of a similar one created in 1934. It was composed of seven judges appointed by the minister of justice for three years. The head of the prosecution of the Cour de cassation presided, and there was one counselor and two avocats généraux of the Cour de cassation, along with three members of the Prosecution Department from the same level as the accused judge. This commission gave advice that was not binding on the minister of justice. If the minister decided on more severe sanctions than those proposed by the commission, an appearance was required before the commission to explain the rationale. The CDP then gave its advice a second time, but the minister of justice made the ultimate decision.

If the Commission de Discipline du Parquet exonerated a judge of the prosecution, the case was referred to a special commission attached to the Cour de cassation. This body was designated each year by the general assembly of the Cour de cassation and was composed of its first president, three counselors and three avocats généraux belonging to that court. The decision of this commission was binding on both the minister of justice and the CDP, but it never heard a case.

The CDP was modified by the organic law of February 25, 1992. The presiding officer remained the same, but the other judges were elected: one judge of the bench and two avocats généraux of the Cour de cassation by their peers; twelve judges belonging to the prosecution and to the administration (at the ministry) by the Collège de magistrats (representative of the judiciary) chosen among the major categories of judges (three of each) so that only the judges of the same rank as the incriminated judge would sit in the CDP; and three from the primary grades of the judiciary. All served for four-year, nonrenewable terms.

When the disciplinary authority, whether the CSM or the minister of justice, concluded that a judge was guilty, the same authority decided what punishment was appropriate. The range of available sanctions was, and still is, considerable and is the same for judges of the bench and of the prosecution, for all are linked to the magistrate's status as a civil servant. That connection is perhaps the most innovative element of the statutory ordinance. article 45 enumerates the sanctions, in order of lesser to greater severity: reprimand with notation in the judge's file, mandatory change of location, withdrawal of certain functions, reduction in grade by one degree, retrogradation, mandatory retirement, and dismissal, with or without pension. A judge's punishment can involve only one sanction unless it is withdrawal of functions, reduction in grade, or retrogradation; in those instances a mandatory change of place can be imposed simultaneously (article 46). A convicted judge can seek an annulment from the Conseil d'Etat.

As all of these procedures have been used, the way they work in practice can be analyzed. From 1959 to May 1, 1994, the final date for the 1958 institution, the CSM had 64 cases brought before it and pronounced punishments 43 times; the CDP was consulted on 23 occasions and advised penalties in 17 cases. The number of cases initiated each year has risen since

1991, even if decisions have not always followed. This imbalance might be explained by the renewed interest in the obligation of reserve and the difficulty of adapting that concept to events. The information given by the Ministry of Justice on the cases themselves concerns the period of 1959–91: 48 judges of the bench and 15 members of the prosecution department have been disciplined. That total of 63 magistrates disciplined must be balanced by awareness that there are approximately 6,000 magistrates in France; moreover, in 32 years each of the 6,000 judgeships could reasonably have been occupied by five people, for a total of around 30,000 magistrates officiating. The proportion of judges whose conduct has been sufficiently egregious to prompt disciplinary procedures is minute by any measure. The figures over the last five years of the period indicate that male magistrates are more likely than their female counterparts to be involved in disciplinary actions: 68 percent of the procedures concerned men, who in 1991 accounted for 57 percent of the magistrature. Information concerning warnings is less complete because the most recent amnesty law, passed on July 20, 1988, expunged from judges' files all notations not related to honor or dignity. Most warnings were not in those categories and have been deleted. Only seven warnings were made from 1988 to 1991.

Disciplinary authorities in France are also known to act quickly. Cases before the CSM have lasted a maximum of 10 months; 26 procedures were settled quite expeditiously—lasting between 7 days and 5 months. Another 14 required 6 to 10 months. The shortest case, the one taking only 7 days, was concluded rapidly because the accused judge appeared to be insane. Procedures against members of the prosecution, heard by the Commission de Discipline du Parquet, have been equally brief. They have ranged from only 14 days to a year, more generally from 2 to 8 months. The longest case, one lasting an entire year, was extended because of disagreements between the minister of justice and the CDP on the appropriate sanction required. Two separate opinions from the CDP were required as a result.

These instances of disciplinary actions cover various types of misconduct proscribed by the codes of behavior in article 43 and also in articles 5, 8, 9, 10, and 13 of the statutory ordinance. The vagueness of the language defining proscribed actions was noted earlier, and even the Ministry of Justice has difficulty in assigning a particular label to some forms of misconduct. It often ignores whether the CSM will retain the basis of accusation or not. The last two cases decided began on the allegation of laziness, but one of them was decided, in 1991, on the grounds of irregular attendance and work. Attitudes toward appropriate conduct also evolve, and what was regarded as a fault even a few years ago might not be treated the same today. In 1974, for example, a *juge d'instruction* who authorized a journalist to be present during a preliminary investigation was found to have violated the secrecy of the investigation and was withdrawn from his functions. On the other hand, in 1991 the minister of justice allowed television cameras to film an entire investigation. The press commented on the event, which was unique.

An overview of all 63 cases of judicial misbehavior suggests that each one is distinctive and bears little resemblance to others. There are, nonetheless, some common elements that permit classification. The disciplinary fault defined in the statutory ordinance of 1958 and the interpretations of it in the commentaries cover the same three facets that have been addressed over the centuries: fault in professional conduct, in private life if notorious, and in political attitude. The bulk of the cases, 34 out of 63, can be classified as professional failings. Some relate to insubordination, others to wrongly dispensing justice (or not dispensing it at all), and a few to abuse of position.

Insubordination was punished on three occasions. The first involved a judge of the bench who, in 1970, refused to exercise the functions of juvenile court judge. Another in 1971 refused to sit for a proceeding, and in 1974 a member of the prosecution refused to take his post. All three magistrates were automatically transferred. One, the judge of the Prosecution Department, refused to acquiesce to the order, and a procedure for abandonment of post was initiated for unilateral breach of contract with the state. This procedure is designed to remove a judge from the administration list but permit payment of the retirement pension if the other requisite conditions are met.

Dispensing justice wrongly or not respecting procedural rules can be punished in various ways, depending on the context and consequences of the judge's actions. Dismissing a suit without an investigation was punished with a reprimand and notation in the judge's file in 1961 (CSM), and the same sanction was applied to a judge who had failed to renew warrants of detention in 1965 (CSM). The judge who had allowed a journalist to cover an investigation was relieved of his functions in 1974 (CSM), as was, the next year, a judge who was negligent concerning detention under remand. Withdrawal of functions can also be coupled with an automatic relocation according to CSM decisions in 1970 and 1990. In the 1970 case, an examining judge had neglected "delays of directions" and had also lunched with a former prisoner. The 1990 decision related to a female magistrate serving as a probationary judge, who had violated procedural rules as well as rules governing the execution of punishment. She had, moreover, established a personal relationship with a prisoner on probation. In these cases the choice of a complementary sanction, a transfer, was justified because both judges had demonstrated a lack of dignity and reserve that was notorious in their private lives. Given that the CSM had regularly changed its membership during the two decades that separated the decisions, the consistency of the punishments strongly points to the continuity that exists within the CSM.

In 1963 a judge was punished for delays in illegal detention during which prisoners had not even been interrogated; the offending magistrate in this case was also charged with absenteeism and serious insufficiency. His punishment was that of "ceasing functions" (CSM), a particularly severe penalty applied when a judge has fewer than 15 years of service and cannot take retirement. The justification for such a harsh decision was that the judge had dispensed justice wrongly and had neglected dispensing it at all.

There are degrees of punitive severity for the failure to dispense justice correctly. Simple professional negligence combined with absenteeism has warranted involuntary transfers in five cases since 1960 (CSM and minister of justice, after advice of CDP). A single variation in the situation may be sufficient to prompt differential treatment, however, as two cases of professional negligence and refusal to respect the obligation of residence illustrate. In 1973 the president of a tribunal de grande instance was punished for two such infractions with loss of his functions as president and with a transfer (CSM). Yet when in 1982 a member of the prosecution was convicted on the same two charges, his penalty was a simple transfer (minister of justice after CDP). That the first judge held the position of president obviously explains the more severe retribution.

But similar offenses have resulted in other penalties. When a decision went against a judge of the bench in 1969 on charges of professional negligence, actions discourteous to the first president of the Court of Appeal, and excessive absence, he was merely reprimanded and received a notation in his file (CSM). A member of the Prosecution Department, on the other hand, who was found to have acted negligently and to have attempted to conceal his absences was reduced in rank and ordered transferred (1968, minister of justice after CDP). A further illustration of how decisions are driven by the specifics surrounding them is the case in 1972 in which a judge of the bench, guilty of professional negligence, requested a transfer, after which the minister of justice revoked the charge.

Another offense is abuse of power, and the sanctions for it tend to be quite severe. A judge in 1959 was retired ex officio for having converted funds to his own use, even though he made restitution (CSM). In 1972 another judge converted funds and overestimated his travel expenses, for which he was removed from office but retained his right to a pension (CSM). A case in 1986 involved a president of a Court of Appeal and two vice-presidents who were found to have taken property (car radios and tape decks) for their personal use that was under seal for various investigations. The president was retired ex officio, and the vice-presidents were automatically transferred (CSM). In 1991 a member of the prosecution was automatically transferred because he had tried to persuade a colleague to be particularly harsh on a young man implicated in a minor offense. The judge's motives were clearly personal as he was trying to prevent the young man from marrying his daughter (minister of justice after CDP). In a rather exceptional case, a judge was removed from office in 1981 because of his generally bizarre behavior; the accusation against him was not tied to any specific incident.

Of course, judges who conduct themselves competently and efficiently in their professional capacities may neglect the most elementary precautions in their private lives. Whereas judges are free to conduct their private lives as they wish, they nevertheless represent their offices and are expected to behave uprightly in public. Some judges are merely imprudent, some are found guilty of committing criminal offenses, and others are "scandalous" in their activities. The parameters of what constitutes scandalous behavior are hardly clear, and examples of judges incurring punishment for it are not helpful because of rules of confidentiality. There are undoubtedly more improprieties in judges' private lives than are ever discovered, but when they come to light the judiciary does not sit passively on the sidelines.

Lack of prudence can take various forms. Being indebted excessively is not in itself reprehensible, but when judges allow debts to reach the point where they cannot be met, they have acted imprudently. In 1965 one judge was automatically transferred for his imprudent indebtedness as well as for his scandalous living (CSM). Another accepted a position on a board of trustees and in doing so violated an article of the statutory ordinance on the incompatibility of holding other offices. In 1972 he was reprimanded and the fact noted in his file (CSM). In 1983 a judge was transferred after kidnapping his own child, who was, by divorce decree, in the custody of the other parent (CSM).

Passing a bad check, in conjunction with maintaining a scandalous life, caused a judge to be ordered in 1962 to "cease his functions" (CSM). In 1969 a retired judge who wrote a worthless check received a penal sanction. Shortly thereafter, the CSM withdrew the honorary title that had been bestowed on him at his retirement. In 1964 another judge was found guilty of robbery; for this his position was revoked and his right to a pension denied (CSM). Another judge violated customs regulations at the frontier in 1970, which prompted the lowering of his rank by one degree (CSM). A judge of the prosecution was found guilty of fraud and was removed from office in 1982 (minister of justice after CDP).

Living a scandalous life, particularly when one is a judge, is regarded as lacking in dignity and honor, and the penalties for it can be harsh. In 1963 a judge was mandatorily retired for breaching the bounds of propriety in his private life (minister of justice after CDP). In 1988 another was retired at age forty for living with a prostitute for whom he had intervened in a legal proceeding, for associating with delinquents, and for purchasing a pistol without a permit and leaving it at a convict's house. The judge in question refused to accept his removal. He married the woman and fought for his reinstatement when he had difficulty earning a living. In February 1993 he appeared on a popular television program, where he revealed his fate; newspaper articles, letters of encouragement, and a support committee resulted. As a consequence, on November 5, 1993, President Mitterrand signed a decree granting personal amnesty, which specified clearly that it obliterated the disciplinary penalty but not the reprehensible facts. The judge was not, therefore, reinstated. However, the judge persisted, and in May 1994 the Ministry of Justice proposed his name for the position of *chargé de mission* for three years at the judicial agency to protect youth (DEJJ). He initially refused but then accepted, regarding the position as the prelude to his reinstatement. This case is unique.

In proceedings against other judges for the conduct of their private lives, allegations have been less serious. In 1980 a judge in a juvenile court established a close relationship with some young drug addicts. Because of her potentially good intentions, she was only withdrawn from the juvenile court and transferred to another location (CSM). The president of a section of a Court of Appeal was demoted to the rank of *conseiller* in 1986 because of his many dubious associations with criminal characters.

A judge can, of course, avoid the humiliation that accompanies a disciplinary proceeding by simply resigning. For example, a judge of the Prosecution Department was accused in 1973 of living a scandalous life, but when he resigned the proceedings were stopped.

The final disciplinary fault is that of failure to follow the obligation of reserve, but it seems to have been the least frequently encountered up to 1991. Only nine such cases occurred, and seven of those involved members of the Prosecution Department. The judges were charged with negative actions toward judicial institutions or the government. In 1963 a judge was mandatorily transferred for attacking the principle of subordination to which all members of the Prosecution Department are subject. He had also attacked the authority of the public prosecutor (minister of justice after CDP). In 1987 a judge who addressed insulting words to the public prosecutor and other authorities was punished by imposed retirement (minister of justice after CDP). The outcomes of these two cases are notably at variance, but presumably the different punishments corresponded to the gravity of the offenses (the specifics of which are confidential). The variance might also be explained by the intervening two decades, during which both attitudes and personnel changed.

A judge of the Prosecution Department in 1975 made such outrageous criticisms of the judicial function that the very legitimacy of the institution was threatened. The minister of justice reprimanded him and ordered a notation in his file. Another judge told reporters in 1976 that his appointment as *procureur de la République* in the town of H—— was a political punishment because he had refused another post offered to him previously. The judge, who never admitted that he had applied for the second position, was held to have discredited the judiciary, for which he was reprimanded with a notation in his file (minister of justice after CDP). The same punishment was given to another judge in 1980 for writing a newspaper article involving the minister of justice (CSM).

Cases having political overtones seem to require more delicacy in their resolution. A judge was charged in 1962 with implicating the government in his judgments, for example, but the CSM found no basis for the allegations. Similarly, in 1987 a member of the prosecution in a public speech attacked the government policy on drug addiction. Much to the relief of both magistrates, the minister of justice decided that they had not transgressed any ethical boundary. In 1978 another disciplinary proceeding had turned out differently: a judge was demoted by one degree in rank and involuntarily transferred for having criticized a government decision on extradition (minister of justice after CDP).

In most of the cases brought against members of the Prosecution Department, the Minister of Justice apparently agreed with the advice of the CDP. In one situation, however, the two diverged. When a judge was charged with making political statements on an illegal radio station, the CDP in 1979 recommended a reprimand, but the minister of justice disagreed. The CDP was approached a second time in 1980 but did not change its recommendation. The minister of justice was, after the second consultation, free to act unilaterally; he ordered a mandatory transfer.

Since 1991, two aspects of the obligation of reserve have again been under discussion: the obligation to keep investigations secret and the obligation to behave neutrally in politics. The French nation is now accustomed to being informed on all government activities, including those of the judiciary. There must be some equilibrium between the public's right to information and the secrecy of investigations; that balance is difficult to find. An administrative note of 1985 authorized the Prosecution Department to inform the press of activities as it deems appropriate, but the judge in charge of the investigation is supposed to maintain confidentiality. During 1993 and 1994, Judge Thierry Jean-Pierre was on the fringe of a disciplinary procedure for cooperating with the press from 1991 through 1993. Then, during the same years, Judge Eric de Montgolfier made headlines for regularly informing the press about the progress of the Valenciennes-Olympique de Marseille football case. He was reminded of his responsibility by President Mitterrand in a public speech in July 1993, and the Ministry of Justice summoned him. The ministry decided at that time to develop a proposal for delineating the relationship between the press and the judiciary. Montgolfier did not change his attitude, and on January 13, 1994, he was ordered by Minister of Justice Pierre Méhaignerie to observe the obligation of reserve or face discipline. The order, although solemn, was not a warning in the legal sense of the term.

Early in 1993, during the campaign for elections for the National Assembly, two judges of the bench, Thierry Jean-Pierre and Jean-Louis Bruguière, participated in a political debate, each supporting a different candidate. Both were reminded of their duty of political reserve. Within a few days, the Ministry of Justice even sent an administrative note to all judges insisting on the obligation of reserve and the necessity of political neutrality.

These cases were reported in the media. Although no disciplinary process ensued, they are illustrative of how disciplinary faults and their punishments are continually adapting.

This summary of disciplinary actions against French judges, of both the bench and the prosecution, may appear to paint an unflattering portrait of the magistrature, but only a small proportion of judges have been found to have breached the professional or personal expectations of their offices. Most judges, having a keen sense of the honor and dignity that accrue to their positions, conform to the long tradition. All French civil servants can be investigated for professional or ethical errors, but there is obviously a greater attentiveness to allegations against judges. Over the centuries there is also a remarkable continuity of ideas about appropriate judicial conduct and about what constitutes a disciplinary fault, even as the contours of those concepts continue to evolve.

Chapter 3

Italy

Maria Elisabetta de Franciscis

Italy is a relatively new state, but one with a long history that is reflected in its approach to questions of judicial ethics and accountability. As early as the Empire of Justinian, government policy defined the proper role and expected behavior of judges—that they act according to the law, without favoritism, and consistent with their consciences. Similarly, the Second Empire constitution enumerated the desired qualities for judges as including fear of God, love of truth, and impartiality.[1] A continuity with those early admonitions can be seen in contemporary Italian practices, though the Roman legacy has been broken and redirected a number of times in the history of the peninsula. The modern Italian state has translated Roman law largely through the French experience, and the current Italian system, which relies on the Consiglio Superiore della Magistratura, or Superior Council of Magistrates (CSM), is a transplantation of the French model, albeit transformed and adapted by the Italian experience.

French influence in Italy results in part from geographic proximity, but even more important was the Napoleonic occupation of the entire peninsula in the early nineteenth century. The Piedmontese constitution of 1848, the Statuto Albertino, that was eventually applied to the unified Italian state, was inspired by the French constitution of 1830.[2] There was, moreover, throughout continental Europe an admiration for and imitation of the Napoleonic system of justice, in which magistrates were instituted as a bureaucracy, part of the apparatus of the state, and the judiciary was divided between ordinary and administrative courts. The Kingdom of Italy repli-

49

cated the Napoleonic conception of the judiciary as a hierarchy, under executive administration that made independence somewhat conditional. The French influence continues; even the 1948 constitution of the Republic of Italy borrows from the constitution of the French Fourth Republic of 1946.[3]

Under the monarchy but before the Fascist era, judicial independence was limited, following the French example of executive dominance and administrative status. Statuto Albertino, article 68, stated that "justice emanates from the King and is administered in his name," and article 73 added that the interpretation of law lay exclusively within the legislative realm. The era from 1861 to 1900 was notable for the lack of any real distinction between politicians and magistrates, as people shifted back and forth between the two arenas. Indeed, half those serving in the Ministry of Justice during that period had held political positions.[4]

The French innovation of a Superior Council of Magistrature was introduced in the Kingdom of Italy in 1907 by the so-called Orlando reform, and its primary role was to protect the independence of the magistrates even though it was an auxiliary to the executive branch and subject to the minister of justice.[5] The council was composed in part of magistrates named by the higher courts and was given limited authority over discipline and promotions. Judges were also granted secure tenure (*inamovibilità*), but could nonetheless be blocked in their careers by promotion, transfer, and discipline decisions. Magistrates in the public ministry, or prosecutors, were not given the same tenure as their counterparts on the bench.[6] The council's powers were widened in 1921 to include administrative control of the judiciary, and security of tenure was extended to the lowest judges (*pretori*).

After Mussolini and the Fascists came to power in 1922, the powers of the CSM were quickly curtailed, first by the Oviglio Act of 1923 and further by the Grandi Law of 1941. Under the latter act, the council was reduced to a committee chaired by the first president of the Corte di Cassazione, along with eight judges appointed by the king on the recommendation of Mussolini and the Grand Fascist Council.[7] The judiciary was kept in check by an infusion of political personnel into its ranks and by various forms of indirect control. The power of the police was increased, and special tribunals separate from the magistrature were created to try political cases. Most magistrates did not protest and few were disciplined; the judicial corps was essentially passive and by 1930, like other state agencies, was infiltrated with Fascists and its basically bureaucratic character reinforced.[8]

A New Superior Council of Magistrates

Mussolini had adeptly manipulated Statuto Albertino, which had been the fundamentally liberal democratic constitution of a constitutional monarchy with limited suffrage. That constitution was necessarily jettisoned when the Constituent Assembly met through 1947 to draft a new republican one, but the new document was not much different structurally from its predecessor. Instead, the major changes were in the nature of underlying principles, civil rights, and political representation. The 1948 constitution, obviously in reaction to the Fascist regime, proclaimed the principle of an independent magistrature by providing in article 101 that "judges are subject only to the law," in article 104 that "the judiciary is an order that is autonomous and independent of all other branches," and in article 107 that "judges may not be removed from office," though a procedure for dismissal in the same article makes the guarantee less than absolute and acknowledges conditions on judicial tenure.

The need for a disciplinary regime had, in fact, been recognized even earlier, and a royal decree issued in the 1946 transitional period had instituted one that remained basically in place until the new Consiglio was implemented in 1958. In some ways, all of the laws that were subsequently passed by the republican government followed the outline of the royal decree and maintained some of its provisions. The royal decree invested judges with secure tenure and provided that those on tribunals and higher courts could not be transferred to different locations or to different functions without their consent. It also set procedures for handling magistrates with permanent physical disabilities, gave the minister of justice the power of surveillance over all magistrates, and enumerated and defined sanctions that could be applied to judges who damaged the trust or compromised the prestige of the ordinary judiciary. That law likewise set procedures for hearings on disciplinary matters under the old Consiglio, including an ultimate appeal to the minister of justice.[9] Later the same year another decree outlined the manner of electing members to the CSM and its disciplinary section (Sezione Disciplinare del CSM).[10]

The 1948 republican constitution formally created a new Consiglio Superiore della Magistratura. Following the French example, the name was carried over, but the institution itself was new. Similarly, the structure, powers, and scope of the new Consiglio are liberally borrowed from the French Fourth Republic constitution. A major deviation lies in the Italian version's clearer separation between the executive and the council.[11] The resulting system led Ehrmann in 1976 to declare that self-administration of the Italian judiciary is "greater than in any other European country."[12] There was a clear determination on the part of the Constituent Assembly, in creating the Superior Council of the Magistrature, to remove control of the judicial apparatus from the executive. One of the early decisions relating to the judiciary was the removal of the minister of justice from the governing body. The vote was split, however, 27 to 17.[13] Rather than moving to a totally autonomous administrative council, the Constituent Assembly chose to create a mixed body in which the magistrates hold a clear majority. There remains, however, a check through the minority participation of legislatively named members. The result of the Constituent Assembly's efforts was a Superior Council of the Magistrature that, according to article 105, "has jurisdiction for employment, assignments and transfers, promotions and disciplinary measures of judges."

In Italy, judicial protection from the executive is more apparent in principle than in practice. The president of the republic presides over the council, and one-third of its elected members are chosen by Parliament. There are several theories about why the Constituent Assembly that wrote the new constitution chose to include the president in the activities of the CSM. Some commentators argue that since the president is the presiding officer of the council, the CSM is a constitutionally recognized branch of government equivalent to the legislative and the executive.[14] A larger number of commentators argue that the council is merely an administrative office and that the presence of the head of state as the presiding officer can be interpreted as a mechanism for protecting participatory democracy, because the president represents and guarantees national unity.[15] Moreover, the vice president, who is elected from among the parliamentary appointees, has in fact typically been the presiding officer.[16]

Additional potential for executive interference in the activities of the council lies in the provision in article 107 that the minister of justice may initiate disciplinary actions against judges. The minister is also given responsibility by article 110 for the organization and operation of those services involved with justice "without prejudice to the Superior Council of the Magistrature." The role of the minister of justice since the Giolittian era (1900–1914) had included administration of the courts, and the same arrangement had been perpetuated and strengthened under the Fascist regime. The Ministry of Justice's prerogatives continued, in matters of judicial personnel management, in tandem with the power of the CSM under the republican constitution, and the ministry's role is, in that sense, an anomaly.[17] Some points of conflict were addressed by the Constitutional Court in 1963, when the court called for cooperation between the bodies,[18] but many overlapping responsibilities persisted as sources of friction. Ministers of justice typically have been jealous of their prerogatives, and conflicts between that office and the CSM are not uncommon. The Constitutional Court became the arbitrator between the two again in 1968. In that instance, the court tried to find a balance by focusing on the dual role of magistrates as both judges and public servants. Magistrates' positions as judges "subject only to the law" under article 101 of the constitution are protected by the CSM, but as civil servants, they are also subject to the same requirements as other government employees under article 97. The latter designation places magistrates under the minister of justice.[19] More recently, the minister attempted to stretch the intent of the Constituent Assembly to imply that both the minister and the CSM must mutually agree on promotions and disciplinary actions. The CSM believed, on the other hand, that it was bound to hear the minister's opinion, but that it was not binding on the council. The court, once again attempting to find a middle ground, and decided that in cases of promotions and disciplinary actions, the CSM should act, but in concert with the minister.[20]

The constitution outlined the basic composition of the council, but left the specifics to Parliament. In addition to the president of the republic, the membership includes by right the first president and procurator general of the highest ordinary court (Corte di Cassazione). The other members, according to article 104, are named two-thirds by the ordinary judges and one-third by Parliament in a joint session. Those elected by Parliament (the lay members) must be full professors of law or lawyers who have been in practice for at least fifteen years. All members of the council serve four-year terms that are not immediately renewable and are prohibited from acting in their professions or serving in Parliament or on regional councils during their terms (article 104).

The new CSM was granted significant powers to administer the judiciary, both bench and prosecution. The only clear constitutional limitation on removal of judges from office is the requirement in article 107 that judicially established rules guaranteeing defense must be observed. The ten constitutional articles that institute the judicial authority and the Superior Council of the Magistrature, despite a fair measure of detail, still required elaboration and definition before the CSM in its new form could begin operation.

The implementing legislation to fill the gaps in the constitutional mandates was not passed until 1958.[21] The judge's union, Associazione Nazionale dei Magistrati Italiani, had resumed operations in 1945. This body was initially composed primarily of judges from the higher grades, who were more conservative and were thus opposed to the new CSM, which was largely free of the minister of justice and of the government. Those judges discreetly delayed the implementing legislation. In the latter half of the 1950s, however, the union's composition altered because of an influx of magistrates from the lower grades who sought innovation and pushed for implementing legislation.[22] The resulting 1958 law failed to satisfy many in the judiciary, because the council was not allowed to try cases that were not initiated by the minister of justice, two-fifths of the *togati* (magistrates, "robed ones") were to be chosen from among members of the Corte di Cassazione (the highest ordinary court), and magistrates were allowed to vote only for the members from their own rank. The members selected by Parliament were required to win a three-fifths majority of the total number of senators and deputies, but in subsequent votes the requirement was only three-fifths of those voting. Only one section of the CSM, the membership of which was explicitly defined, was to deal with disciplinary hearings, and the president of the republic was barred from presiding over those deliberations; the vice president of the council alone could chair disciplinary matters.

As the Consiglio has evolved, its political nature has become increasingly more apparent. The Italian political system has been given the pejorative label of *partitocrazia*, or government by the parties. Most positions in government and the parastate agencies are distributed according to party affiliations and ties to party leadership.[23] This results in a system of *lottizzazione*, or allocation among the parties. It is a patronage process whereby jobs, political positions, and a variety of other valuable functions are apportioned among the major parties in a rough approximation of their relative electoral popularity.[24] The parliamentary appointments to the CSM are, not surprisingly, subject to the same distribution formula. The Christian Democrats name four and the Democratic Party of the Left (former Communist Party) receives three, while the smaller Socialist Party has two and the Liberal Party, one.[25] Electoral reforms passed in 1993 completely reconfigured the parties, and a new line-up appeared after the 1994 elections. The continuance of the *lottizzazione* in some form is likely, but the players will undoubtedly be different.

The politicization of the CSM can also be seen in the relationship that has developed between it and the president of the republic. The president presides, as noted previously, when the council sits as a whole; the president also convenes its meetings and sets or approves its agendas. The vice president serves as chair in the president's absence and presides over the disciplinary section. The vice president is, by definition, a political rather than a judicial figure who, though elected by the council as a whole, must be one of the parliamentary designees. The limits of the vice president's powers in relation to the president's became an issue during the presidential term of Francesco Cossiga (1985–92), who was himself a constitutional law professor and former prime minister. He was often engaged in a public conflict with the CSM, and the Constitutional Court was finally called upon to resolve the attribution of powers controversy. The court's conclusion was that the vice president is allowed to act in the president's absence, but this does not imply any honorary attribution of powers.[26]

A number of thorny issues were ignored or sidestepped by the originators of the new council, and even the parliamentary act of 1958 that finally implemented the CSM left a number of ambiguities and gaps in the definition of its operations. Controversy has arisen over some of those undefined areas such as the use of committees. The implementing legislation mentions that the CSM may use investigative committees to smooth the work of the larger group, and it specifically created two committees, one for appointments to higher courts and another for disciplinary measures. The president subsequently formed a number of other committees and made appointments to them. Another touchy issue was the question of a disciplinary committee, because article 105 of the constitution places the authority for disciplinary action in the CSM itself, not in an internal committee. The Constitutional Court finally resolved the controversy by deciding that such a committee was in fact constitutional but that it must be formed in accordance with the proportionality of representation of the larger group.[27] Nine members of the CSM form the disciplinary committee, and six additional members are elected as substitutes. The composition of that body was altered to meet the distribution of the CSM *in plenum*. The eight members, in addition to the presiding officer, are as follows: two elected from among the legislative appointees, two from the highest ordinary court, one from an appellate court, two from tribunals, and one from among the remaining categories.

The Disciplinary Process

Most activities of the Superior Council of the Magistrature are purely administrative; discipline, the exception, is a jurisprudential activity. The discipline committee of the CSM serves as both judge and jury. The magistrate whose behavior is in question has been allowed to have counsel to aid in his defense since a Constitutional Court decision in 1968. That decision specifically permitted an accused judge to be assisted by another magistrate.[28] The prosecutor before the committee is the prosecutor general of the Corte di Cassazione.

A magistrate can be prosecuted for allegations of criminal wrongdoing and, since 1988, can also be liable civilly. There are, however, offenses that are peculiar to the magistrature that can bring accusations before the CSM. A magistrate may be formally investigated for failure in duties or for behavior that damages the public image of the profession or compromises the prestige of the judiciary. These ambiguous terms seem to correspond roughly to French requirements that magistrates violate neither the dignity nor the honor of their offices. Damaging the public image of the judiciary has been defined, however, as including violations of professional ethics relative to the time and style of work or relative to relationships with the parties to cases, experts before the court, colleagues, or the press. Compromising the prestige of the judiciary involves violation of professional ethics relating to credibility, conflicts of interests, and abuse of power.[29] In addition, a magistrate can be censored for violating the residency requirement[30] or leaving the precinct without the permission of the official hierarchically superior.[31] Some of these requirements, including the last, are taken directly from prerepublican laws, but they all have some antecedent in earlier eras. And, as in previous times, these prescriptions and prohibitions suffer from an intrinsically obscure quality.[32]

Proceedings before the disciplinary committee approximate those of a criminal process: first, there is an investigation or judicial inquiry, which is followed by a hearing. The request for an investigation may come from the minister of justice or from the prosecutor general of the highest ordinary court. The minister of justice, however, must formally make a request to the prosecutor general, who then may choose to ask the CSM to begin either a formal investigation or a summary procedure. If the prosecutor general selects the second route, he must inform the minister of justice and explain his rationale 10 days before proceeding with a summary procedure. The accused judge must also be informed of both the charges and the investigation. At the conclusion of the investigatory stage, the prosecutor general must report his findings to the disciplinary section of the CSM. At this point the committee deliberates in chambers and the process can be stopped only by unanimous agreement that the evidence does not support the charges by both the committee and the prosecutor. Otherwise, a date will be set for a hearing, and both the accused judge and the prosecutor must be notified of it at least 10 days in advance. There are two other relevant time limits that must be met: the hearing must occur within one year's time from the beginning of the investigation, and a verdict must be rendered within the following two years. The entire process is invalidated if these deadlines are not met, unless the accused judge specifically requests extensions.[33]

The presiding official in the disciplinary committee must decide whether or not to bring to the formal hearing the witnesses and experts who were heard during the investigation. The accused judge has the right to be informed about the findings and to be present at the hearings. Hearings take place behind closed doors and, where applicable, the processes of a formal criminal trial are followed. The accused also has the final word that concludes the hearings. The secrecy that cloaks hearings denies any insight into the specific nature of the process or of the evidence that may or may not be considered. One assumes that evidentiary rules akin to those in criminal trials prevail. Immediately following the close of the hearings, the committee convenes to deliberate, without the presence of the prosecutor. Any decision of the committee must be accompanied by an explanation, and copies are forwarded to the minister of justice, the prosecutor general and the accused magistrate. Decisions of the committee may be appealed to the highest ordinary court, the Corte di Cassazione.

A number of sanctions are available to the CSM, and they vary according to the gravity of the charges. Again, some continuity with earlier practices is reflected in the disciplinary measures available to the council. Admonitions, censures, loss of seniority, and removal and dismissal were specifically listed in the 1946 royal decree that preceded the republican constitution.[34] Three new sanctions are currently available to the CSM—loss of salary, involuntary transfer, and exemption from office. The mildest sanction is the admonition, which can be imposed without a proceeding before the CSM. An admonition is, as the word implies, an oral reprimand given to a judge by a superior. The superior judge must notify both the CSM and the minister of justice, and the judge who was admonished may, within 30 days, request a disciplinary investigation by the CSM. The remaining punishments all require a decision by the CSM, and some are used in conjunction with specific forms of misbehavior. Loss of salary is, for example, the penalty imposed on a magistrate who has violated the residency obligation. In this case, the offending magistrate's salary is withheld for a period equivalent to the time the judge was illegally absent.

The least severe sanction that can result from a finding of culpability by the Superior Council is a censure and, unlike an admonition, it is a formal, written condemnation of a judge's behavior. An involuntary transfer is the next level of sanction that can be applied to a judge who the CSM has found to have violated ethical requirements. Loss of seniority is an even more severe punishment, particularly since promotions are no longer based on merit but on seniority alone.[35] A magistrate may forfeit between two months and two years of seniority, which has the effect of postponing promotion to a higher rank or to a higher court. The new placement of the offending magistrate on the seniority list is determined by the Superior Council and may not be lower than the fortieth or higher than the tenth of the positions available in the next rank. Magistrates who have been censured or who have been given a reduction in seniority are also not eligible for election to the CSM, except when the censure occurred more than 10 years earlier and was not followed by any additional actions by the council.

Exemption from office can be imposed when the council does not find sufficient evidence of a magistrate's misbehavior to require a formal sanction but is nevertheless convinced that the magistrate no longer has the public's confidence. Whereas removal and dismissal are final, an exemption is temporary and lasts only as long as the case is underway or for a specified period of loss of salary. The magistrate's loss of trust must be such that, according to the findings of the CSM, it will adversely affect the professional performance of the judge. The most drastic action that the council can take against an offending magistrate is dismissal or removal from office for commission of a major infraction; judges are otherwise guaranteed secure tenure. Dismissal is automatic when a judge is found guilty of a criminal offense or is imprisoned for a premeditated crime. Otherwise, a full investigation and hearing before the CSM are required. Both dismissal and removal are executed by a decree from the president of the republic countersigned by the minister of justice.

The record of the Superior Council of the Magistrature is a mixed one. Though it was given broad powers for personnel management by the constitution and in subsequent implementing legislation, the CSM has not applied this authority evenly. In its early years it was instrumental in ending practices carried over from the Fascist era, in particular the maintenance of dossiers on magistrates' personal and public conduct. The CSM purged all information of that nature from personnel files and established strict rules governing what type of information could be collected thereafter. The CSM actually plays only a minor role in promotion and advancement, since seniority has replaced merit.

Information on activities of the CSM is spotty and difficult to obtain, partially because of the rules of confidentiality. The various procedural phases also confuse attempts to describe the situation in the aggregate, and reports of the disposition of charges against a single magistrate by the disciplinary section of the CSM may include multiple verdicts and sanctions. Moreover, in the four years to the end of 1975, eighteen decisions were being reconsidered because of previously excluded evidence, correction of errors, or reexaminations. As a result, the appearance of some cases in more than one year inflates the number of cases. The statistics and facts that are revealed are only those that the disciplinary section chooses to release.[36] The picture, in other words, is less than complete.

Giuseppe Di Federico's examination of the period from 1957 to 1974 found that only seven magistrates were removed for mental or physical infirmity. More striking, however, during those 17 years only four cases, out of 192 investigations and hearings, resulted in the removal from office of the magistrates.[37] In the period 1972 to 1975, CSM disciplinary activity increased, and 116 procedures were begun. Of those that were concluded, 23 resulted in provisional suspensions from active service and loss of salaries. The 192 magistrates involved in the charges during 1957–74 came from all judicial ranks, from the lowest to the highest: 5 auditor judges (the first probationary service in the magistrature), 23 assistant judges, 77 major trial judges (*tribunale*), 85 appellate level magistrates, and five *cassazione* (highest ordinary court) magistrates. During that time 40 cases were concluded in favor of the accused magistrates because the facts alleged could not be proved (8), evidence was insufficient (13), or the allegations did not involve a prohibited activity (19). The last category is most closely associated with what are labeled "frivolous" complaints in the United States. Notably, 14 cases were dropped because of failure to meet the statutorily prescribed deadlines, and 3 were closed because of the deaths of the accused magistrates. Sixteen other magistrates resigned from their offices after the inquiries began, and the CSM classified those cases as closed.

Only 37 judges were actually found culpable and punished. The specific charges against them are not public information, but the CSM's own data clearly demonstrate that a single ethical infraction is not sufficient to trigger a serious penalty. Of those found guilty of one violation, ten were given

admonitions and three were censured. Magistrates violating multiple prohibitions were punished more harshly—three were removed, one was dismissed, and two lost their seniority. Removal occurs only when involvement in business activities results in unmanageable indebtedness to a
lawyer or to someone who has a criminal background; when excessive debt
is the result of gambling; or when the magistrate has business or social relationships with mafia figures.[38]

The caseload of the CSM has increased dramatically, while its inclination to impose penalties on magistrates remains disproportionately restrained. In 1990 the council had 1,605 cases, of which 352 were decided and
93 reached the disciplinary committee. In the cases that were heard, 22
magistrates were found not guilty, and 16 received some form of punishment. Ten were admonished, and one was censured. Four lost their seniority, one was dismissed, and seven who were found guilty of infractions
resigned, thereby forestalling any disciplinary actions. The remaining 48
cases either had not been concluded or were under reconsideration at the
conclusion of the year.[39]

In 1991 the CSM disciplinary section decided only 59 cases, out of an unknown number of complaints received. One case was dismissed for failure
to meet the statutory deadlines, and another because the accused judge resigned. The major cause for dismissal was that the accusation did not involve prohibited behavior (21 cases), but 5 decisions exonerated the accused magistrates, and 4 others were dismissed for unspecified reasons. Of
the accused judges found culpable, one lost seniority and was transferred,
and 13 were censured. In 13 other cases, the magistrates' behavior was
deemed to constitute an unlawful act (*sussistenza di illecito*), but no sanctions were reported.[40]

The CSM publishes selected decisions in a journal distributed only to
magistrates. Names, locations, and all other information that might iden-
tify the magistrates involved are carefully concealed. Only a brief summary
of the alleged offense and the punishment are reported, presumably for the
purpose of apprising magistrates of how specific types of conduct have
been interpreted as breaching the bounds of ethical behavior. For our purposes, these abbreviated judgments permit some insights into the thinking
of the disciplinary section of the CSM. A prosecutor (*sustituto procuratore*)
received a classic Mercedes automobile worth more than $100,000 as a gift
from a local businessman. The prosecutor was not found to have acted on
any matter in his official capacity that involved the businessman, and his
conduct was entirely in the realm of private behavior. The CSM concluded

nonetheless that acceptance of such a lavish present created a favorable disposition that might affect future official actions. It was, in effect, an illegal gratuity because of the presumed assumption on the part of the giver that the magistrate would be inclined to repay the gesture at some unspecified future time. The magistrate was punished with the loss of two years of seniority, a transfer of duties, and a geographic transfer.[41]

A magistrate was censured for arbitrating a communal matter and conferring with the mayor and other figures who were implicated in a criminal investigation. The CSM censured the magistrate for compromising the trust and credibility of the magistrature. Its rationale was that the appearance of objectivity and impartiality could no longer be assured. Another prosecutor was exonerated of any unethical actions in sending a letter to the president of his section and to the presiding public minister regarding a criminal investigation. His letter recommended that a prosecution be dropped. It was motivated, according to the CSM, solely by his belief that the accused was not guilty. The magistrate had, moreover, removed himself from involvement in the case.[42]

One can extrapolate from the information available that very few magistrates are ever discovered engaging in illicit conduct or punished for such by the Superior Council of the Magistrature. The argument could be offered that the magistrature in Italy is of such quality, in terms of both ethics and competence, that few require discipline. As alluring as that proposition may be, the sheer number of complaints—almost one for every four magistrates in 1990—suggests that something else is at work. Because the activities of the CSM, its investigations, hearings, and deliberations, are cloaked in secrecy, one can only speculate about the possible reasons for the substantial gulf between the large number of allegations and the few instances of discipline.

The potential explanations for the discrepancies are the same ones that lie at the base of the entire issue of judicial accountability in a democracy. Judicial independence requires that judges be free from executive and legislative interference and be protected from influences exerted by interest groups and and other external interests. This independence may, though, relate to the judiciary as a whole or to a single judge. How is a judge to defend against unjustified accusations? The Superior Council of the Magistrature, as the body that receives and hears complaints about judicial behavior, is designed to shield the accused magistrate as well as to police unethical conduct.[43] The secrecy that shrouds its proceedings serves to screen the judge who is the subject of baseless accusations from professional or personal humiliation. But that system can be a double-edged sword; secrecy, together with the few instances in which judges are found wanting by their colleagues, can give the impression that magistrates pull the curtain to cover up ethical lapses within their ranks.

The CSM has been the object of frequent criticism for its obvious politicization, for the insularity of the judiciary, and for its skewed representation of different ranks of the magistrature. One means for dealing with the persistent dissatisfaction was to rewrite legislation regulating the CSM, once in 1976 and again in 1990. Both new laws aimed at altering the mode of electing individuals to the council. The 1976 legislation added auditor judges (the beginning position in the judicial hierarchy) to those who were entitled to vote, and it clarified and opened up the processes by which the judicial representatives to the council were to be elected.[44] The 1990 reform altered the constituencies from which the judicial representatives were to be elected by their peers. Four territorial colleges replaced the original system of votes according to rank and fixed the number of seats allocated to each of the four regions.[45] Even those two reform attempts, however, have failed to stem the tide of negative commentary about the current system.

Civil Liability

Public support for the Italian magistrature is mercurial, rising and falling dramatically in a short space of time. Judges in the Fascist period quietly complied with dictates of the authoritarian regime; the judiciary failed to serve as the bulwark against repressive government actions, as liberal democratic theory would prescribe. Italy, unlike the Federal Republic of Germany, never underwent "de-fascification" after the war, and the judges under Mussolini's regime retained their positions under the republican constitution until death or retirement removed them from the ranks of the magistrature. The low esteem in which they were held was demonstrated in the debates of the Constituent Assembly over adopting judicial review. One reason for the creation of the Constitutional Court, distinct from the remainder of the judiciary, was to avoid placing the power to review legislation in the hands of holdover Fascist judges. One explanation for the delay in passing the implementing legislation for the CSM is the control that these judges held over the higher courts and the judge's union, the National Association of Magistrates. Only in 1956 was a new generation of magistrates able to seize control of the union and then to make a concerted push for creation of the long-delayed CSM.

The 1970s, the "years of lead" when terrorism crippled Italy, saw a new prestige attach to the judiciary. Judges and prosecutors formed on the front lines of the war against terrorists, and many were themselves targets of attacks. Magistrates were elevated to the status of national heroes. That prestige waned rapidly with the disclosure that several judges and one ranking member of the CSM were on the membership lists of the illegal and sinister P-2 Masonic Lodge. In 1986 a former president of the criminal court in Catania was charged with attempting to influence the outcome of an organized crime investigation. The public's regard for the judicial profession fell so low that two referenda were proposed to limit its power. One proposal, for which the requisite 500,000 voter signatures were obtained, called for popular election of members of the CSM; that referendum was blocked by the Constitutional Court.[46] A second proposal, however, reached the voters and passed by an overwhelming majority of 80 percent. Introducing another sanction for erring judges, it revoked the shield from civil liability for judges that had been recognized in Italy since 1865.[47]

Specifically, the referendum proposal asked the Italian public, albeit in rather confusing language, whether judges should pay damages caused in cases of serious negligence. Parliament passed a law in 1988 to implement the sense of the referendum results.[48] If a magistrate, in his official duties, committed fraud or made a serious error, the aggrieved party could seek compensation from the state for financial damages or loss of liberty. The admissibility of the complaint is determined by the tribunal that is closest to the location where the original proceedings took place. There are separate procedures in the appellate courts that follow rules of civil procedure to award damages, which cannot exceed one-third of the offending magistrate's net annual salary at the time the error was committed. The judge is not a party per se to the proceedings but may be present and intervene at any stage. Disciplinary actions can also be pressed against the magistrate, but these are different from those pursued before the CSM and may involve monetary compensation.

The Constitutional Court in 1990 invalidated a portion of the new legislation that would have allowed limited retroactivity.[49] At the same time, it upheld the use of the tribunal where the alleged offense occurred to certify the admissibility of the civil liability question. The court explained that a filter was necessary to prevent, among other things, procedures designed to intimidate magistrates and thereby interfere with their independence. Even under the interpretation offered by the Constitutional Court, the law has been criticized as creating a practical problem of operation and a situation of considerable uncertainty.[50]

Politics and Accountability

Frequent reference to the "crisis" of the judiciary in Italy relates to a variety of failings attributed to it. One problem, not restricted by any means to Italy, is that of balancing judicial independence and autonomy with the powers of the other branches of government.[51] The problem has multiple aspects, but the CSM is at "the eye of the cyclone," being frequently criticized for its excessive politicization.[52] The CSM is obviously political in the sense that the parliamentary designees are named for their party affiliation by a political branch of government. Their presence gives a political character to undertakings of the body, but it is not the only source. The Italian judiciary is itself a highly politicized group. The representation of divergent persuasions on the bench has been hailed as reflecting the pluralism that exists in Italian society. The manifestations are more dramatic than the pluralism label suggests.

Italian magistrates are members of unions that represent different political positions. The National Association of Magistrates (ANM), which originally blocked implementation of the CSM and later supported it, split in 1960. The next year a competitor, Unione Magistrati Italiani, or UMI, of a far more conservative bent, was formed. Schisms within the moderate-to-liberal ANM led to its demise and the creation of two additional unions, one more leftist (Magistratura Democratica, or MD) and one more centrist (Terzo Potere, or TP). This splintering and reformation within the magistrature continued in a somewhat regular cycle until by 1989 four unions of distinctly differing political persuasions emerged: MD on the left; Movimento per la Giustizia, left-center; Unità per la Costituzione, center; and Magistratura Indipendente, right. By 1990 even the Greens were represented. The mere existence of unions for magistrates might suggest an unacceptable level of politicization, but the French magistrature is also unionized. What makes the Italian situation particularly troubling is the overt political affiliations of each union. The judicial members of the CSM run on their union affiliations, and their electors apparently follow union lines in voting. More than the general political inclinations of the unions are reflected in this process; each union also espouses a position on the appropriate goals and roles of the CSM. Should that body be a shield against external pressures, or should it work to secure the tradition of qualifications for members of the magistrature?[53] A corollary question is the precise nature of the CSM. One response is that it is merely a magistrates' union, a type of pluralistic cabinet to govern the judges.[54]

The council is highly politicized in its selection of both internal and external appointees, but it is charged with impartially administering and policing the ranks of some 7,000 magistrates. The group that the council oversees scores very differently with the public from year to year. The magistrature was held in such disrepute in 1984 that 28 percent of the public had no trust in it, but its work was once again receiving high marks in 1993, when negative reactions to it had shrunk to only 13.5 percent.[55] The task of the CSM has become even more complicated since Parliament chose to combat organized crime and terrorism by giving the magistrature some extraordinary powers to investigate often ill-defined crimes. Magistrates were authorized to use preventive detention as a tool against terrorists in the 1970s. That tactic was intended to keep terrorists from fleeing or from committing additional crimes, but it was typically more effective as a means of "encouraging" those detained to implicate others. Those who became informers in exchange for freedom, reduced sentences, or even a type of lucrative witness protection program were called *pentiti,* or repenters. A pervasive question in Italy is the veracity of testimony gained through such tactics.[56]

Similar methods were used in the 1980s against alleged organized crime figures and most recently against some 3,000 politicians and businessmen in political corruption cases. Magistrates have also been given the power to prosecute individuals charged with the ambiguous crime of "criminal associations," a prerogative that permits a dangerous enlargement of the whole criminal process, often based only on the slender evidence provided by pentiti.[57] The only monitor on magistrates' use or abuse of these powerful prerogatives is the highly politicized CSM.

The magistrature in Italy, like the political system itself, has dubious credibility. The magistrates in Milan who pursued political corruption and kickback schemes in the *mani pulite,* or clean hands, investigation were granted the same hero status that was once given to the magistrates who defeated the terrorists. Simultaneously, however, the president of the criminal section of the highest ordinary court was under investigation on serious corruption charges; the CSM, in this highly publicized case, withdrew him from hearing cases and cut his salary in half pending the outcome of investigations.[58] Likewise, the highest ranking judge of the Milan tribunal was under investigation for having shown favoritism to the late Raul Gardini, head of the massive Enimont empire. Forty other magistrates have been accused of illegal membership in the Masonic lodge,[59] and a further 40 for complicity ranging from ignoring corruption schemes to aiding such schemes in the programs to rebuild earthquake-ravaged areas in Campania and Lucania.[60] Judges who allegedly acted in tandem with the kickback and bribery schemes of politicians and businessmen, nicknamed *magistratopoli*, were also under investigation.[61]

Calls for reform of the CSM are, not surprisingly, being raised yet again. One set of proposals that predates the latest series of scandals was offered by an ad hoc presidential committee in February 1991. Obviously, one of the first recommendations is that political influence be minimized by decreasing the size of the CSM to perhaps 12 members and by assigning disciplinary matters to a separate committee of magistrates who are not part of the CSM. Parliamentarians would be stopped from seeking positions on the CSM, and CSM magistrates from seeking parliamentary posts. The current system allows, if not encourages, use of a position on the Superior Council to gain political visibility and higher political office. These reforms or others along the same line could be accomplished through the difficult process of constitutional revision or through the less onerous approach of revising thoughtfully and thoroughly the legislation that now governs the CSM.[62] Gaps and lacunae exist, as the revisions since 1958 have been ad hoc and piecemeal. A coherent and unified law to fill in the gaps would help solve the Italian dilemma of protecting judicial independence and supervising judicial accountability by means of the highly partisan and politicized Superior Council of the Magistrature.

Chapter 4

England

The judicial system of England and Wales has evolved in an almost unbroken fashion since the Norman invasion more than 900 years ago. Norms governing judicial accountability and judicial independence, although now quite opposite to medieval practices, changed gradually and without dramatic interruption. Even the civil war in the mid–seventeenth century left the judiciary and the rules governing the tenure of judges largely intact. Judges were formerly clearly the Crown's judges, serving *durante beneplacito nostro* (during our good pleasure), and royal control of judges reached its apex under the Stuarts in the seventeenth century. A backlash against royal interference in the administration of justice led to the change to tenure *quamdiu se bene gesserint* (so long as he does well), and English judges are now perhaps the most independent of any in the Western world. Indeed, no judge has been removed from a higher court since 1830, and an independent judiciary is valued in England as essential "if application is made to the courts to check administrative authorities from exceeding their powers and to direct the performance of duties owed by public officials to private citizens."[1]

A number of anomalies distinguish the English experience from that of other European nations. The status and protections of the judiciary, like those of Parliament and the Crown, have gradually flowered and developed; shifts of power and prerogative occurred piecemeal, largely separated from specific climactic events. The basis of English law is, moreover, common rather than civil, and it was not extended to the whole of the

United Kingdom. Only England and Wales share a common legal system, as Scotland maintained its more Roman-based tradition and Northern Ireland follows a separate model. Britain has a flexible and unwritten constitution, and courts may not, as a result, rule on the constitutional validity of legislation. Nonetheless, the judicial power is apparent in interpretation of statutes and application of the common law.

Sir Francis Bacon described English judges in the early seventeenth century as lions, "but yet lions under a throne, being circumspect that they do not check or oppose any points of sovereignty."[2] Dependence on the monarch characterized judges until 1761, and even now the courts are denied the authority to intrude into the sovereignty of Parliament. The difference lies in where sovereignty is placed. The differentiation of executive and legislative functions changed through a long history, and that, not the demarcation between executive and judicial activities, has governed the place of judicial power. Judges continue to be the Crown's judges, even though a strict separation is observed once a judge is appointed. A continuity with the past is seen, as it was in France and Italy, in the English approach to judicial independence; the differences can be found largely in the English propensity to create new labels while retaining the previous system, while the French and Italians tended to retain the names of institutions but to alter both the form and substance.

Norman through Tudor Periods

There were no professional lawyers or judges at the time of the Norman conquest in 1066, but, even so, a book of English law, *The Laws of Henry,* was compiled as early as 1115. Instead of professional judges, groups of suitors whose only qualification was ownership of land decided cases in county courts. Royal courts then began extending their jurisdiction, and professional judges became essential. In 1178 Henry II appointed judges called commissioners in Oyer and Terminer and also appointed officials from his household to serve the judicial function in the *curia regis* (the king's inner council). These early judges were clergy, not trained in law, and their salaries were so small that fees from litigants comprised a large part of their income. Only with the signing of the Magna Carta in 1215 was the king obliged to appoint judges (justices, constables, sheriffs, and bailiffs) from among those who "know the law and mean duly to serve it." A professional judiciary dates from shortly thereafter, in the reign of Henry III.

Nonetheless, corruption scandals tainted the courts, and Chief Justice Thorpe was hanged for bribery in 1350. So great was the incidence of bribery in the judiciary that a statute was passed to punish the convicted offender by means of a fine three times the bribe and permanent discharge from the king's service, as well as whatever additional punishments the king might impose.[3] Another chief judge of the King's Bench was punished with a stiff fine, while the chief justice of the Court of Common Pleas was compelled to flee the country. Other judges confronted public wrath. Lord Chancellor Simon de Sudbury in 1381 was pursued by an angry crowd that beheaded him, and the next year Lord Chief Justice Cavendish was subjected to a mock trial and executed by another mob.[4]

By the end of the thirteenth century, guilds of lawyers formed the Inns of Court to train for the practice of law,[5] a step intended to lend some professional legitimacy to the bench and the bar. During this era and for almost the next 400 years, judges remained insecure in their tenure: "they held their office at the pleasure of the monarch and lost it at the moment of his death."[6]

Judges were not subject, though, to discipline or removal only by the king. They were caught in the twin political pincers of the king, who could remove, and Parliament, that could impeach. Impeachment originated in a crude form in 1376 and was the political tool of Parliament against officials of the monarch, including judges. In 1386 the House of Commons accused the lord chancellor, Sir Michael de la Pole, of seven specific offenses: four involved dereliction of duty and three, peculation or embezzlement. He was condemned by the Lords, ordered to prison pending the payment of a fine, and land and profits were confiscated. The king, however, pardoned the lord chancellor and returned him to royal service.[7]

King Richard II, seeking to avoid similar attacks on his ministers in the future, consulted a group of judges and serjeants (forerunners of lawyers) about whether Parliament could impeach an officer of the Crown without the king's permission. The legal opinion was that Parliament could not do so, for no prosecution could go forward to which the king was not a party. Parliament on March 2, 1388, accused and impeached the judges who had given the king this advice. The House of Lords convicted and sentenced them to death by drawing and hanging; only the intervention of the clergy on their behalf spared their lives.[8]

Judges chose, despite their position in the king's service, to remain on the political sidelines for a while thereafter. They were particularly cautious during the War of the Roses (1455–71), even when the House of Lords requested an authoritative answer to the question of the Duke of York's claims to the throne. The royal judges and the king's serjeant declined, stating that the issue was not a matter of law. During this period, they similarly refused a proposal to define the limits of parliamentary prerogative and steered a narrowly drawn course between the competing houses of York and Lancaster.[9]

When the Tudors ascended the throne in 1485, they attempted to systematize law and its enforcement throughout the country. Impeachment fell into disuse, replaced by bills of attainder, whereby conviction and sentencing depended on a single parliamentary vote. Though this was an era of considerable upheaval and vengeance and judges continued to serve only at the pleasure of the monarch, the bench tended to act independently and apolitically. The judges, if the situation required it, were even known to criticize executive actions. These early assertions of judicial integrity and nonpartisanship won judges a high level of esteem.

Judges under the Stuarts

The Stuart era (1603–88) was violent and volatile, punctuated with civil war. The early Stuart period was marked by a monarchal attempt to press both divine right and absolutism to extremes. The effect of these goals was evident in the judiciary, since the judges were, after all, the king's men and serving only at his will.[10] The rule governing the tenure of judges was clear: *durante beneplacito nostro,* or *during our good pleasure.* An officeholder who was dismissed could, in theory at least, sue for a writ of *scire facias* to require the king to show cause. Chief Baron Fleming attempted this strategy in 1629, and Charles I responded by suspending him for life.[11]

One of the first judges to lose the king's pleasure in this period was Sir Edward Coke. In the *Case of the Commendams* in 1616, the king's right to grant a *commendam* was challenged. James I had granted to Bishop Neile of Lincoln two benefices to be held in commendam, or together with his bishopric. Two individuals challenged the legality of that action and the king's power to make such a grant. The king instructed Coke and the other judges not to hear the case, because it was a challenge to royal prerogative. They replied that their oaths of office required them to ignore the royal order. When summoned by the king, however, all but Coke agreed to comply with the royal command. Coke was censured for his stubbornness and later dismissed from office.[12] No one seemed to be alarmed, though, that the king would rid himself of an impertinent judge. Coke, in fact, joined the Privy Council later and then pursued a career in the royal court.[13]

Sir Edward Coke was not the only notable judge to lose his office. Sir Francis Bacon, lord chancellor, was impeached and removed by Parliament in 1620. He was accused of bribery and corruption in chancery suits. He confessed that he had indeed accepted gifts from people whose cases were before him, but that the gifts had had no effect on his judgment. Indeed, in a number of cases his decisions went against those from whom he had received gratuities. The Lords accepted his admission of guilt and, to his surprise, exacted a substantial fine, imprisoned him in the Tower of London at the king's pleasure, and banned him from holding public office again. The king remitted the fine, and Bacon's time in the Tower lasted only about four days. He was also granted a general pardon in 1621. That year another judge, Sir John Bennet of Canterbury, was charged by the Commons with bribery and corruption. The Lords did not try that case, which was pursued in the Star Chamber; Bennet was convicted and punished with a heavy fine.[14]

Charles I, who succeeded James in 1625, was even more bent on absolutism, trying to control his judges and to rule without interference from Parliament. The judges seemed willing to comply with the wishes of a king who had said, in a speech to Parliament, that to the judges alone, *"under me,* belongs the interpretation of the laws [emphasis mine]." The judiciary enjoyed its comforts and its honors and chose to stand clear of the battles between the Crown and Parliament. Any judges who might have doubted that their loyalty was to the king, were reminded of it clearly when the chief baron of the Exchequer was suspended in 1629, and the chief justice of Common Pleas, Sir Robert Heath, was dismissed in 1634.[15]

The king dissolved Parliament in 1629 and did not reconvene it until his need for revenue pressed heavily in 1640. The reputation of the judiciary during this era sank, as independence was undermined by frequent dismissals and new royal appointments acquiesced totally to the king's whims. Corruption and bribery were not unknown on the royal courts.[16] The king adopted a procedure of consulting with the judges before undertaking questionable actions, thereby prejudicing their position before the issue could be raised in a court of law. A glaring example of this was the case of *Rex v. Hampden,* known as the "ship money case." The king consulted with his judges before issuing writs of ship money, which demanded ships from his subjects, in 1634 and again in 1635. The king asserted that the existence of an emergency allowed him to raise such "taxes" without the consent of Parliament. Hampden argued that no emergency had existed from 1634 to 1635 and that Parliament could have been summoned to issue the writs. The decision in the case, when heard by the 12 judges of the Exchequer Chamber, supported the king's position, although five of the judges ruled in favor of Hampden. The judgment in favor of the king severely undercut the authority of Parliament. As Sir Robert Berkeley explained the court's position in 1638, "*Rex is lex*, for he is *lex loquens*, a living, a speaking, an acting law," and "the king cannot do wrong."[17] Parliament was reconvened, and in 1641 it impeached Lord Chief Justice Bramston, Lord Chief Baron Davenport, and Mr. Justice Sir Robert Berkeley, along with other judges who had supported the king in the ship money case.[18] The civil war followed the next year, and the interregnum continued until the ascension of Charles II in 1660.

The king was forced in 1641 to accept new terms for judicial tenure: quamdiu se bene gesserint, or during good behavior. Under this prescription, Lord Chief Justice Keeling was called before the Commons for "severe and illegal fining and imprisoning juries." He had allegedly even defamed the Magna Carta by saying, "Magna Farta? what ado with this have we?"[19] He offered his defense before the Commons, who debated for four hours before deciding to make the fining and imprisonment of jurors illegal, but not to continue impeachment actions against Keeling.[20]

The next year Charles II reverted to the practice of dismissing or suspending judges at his pleasure.[21] This power was exercised arbitrarily, politically, or indeed without reason. The public, however, was not necessarily concerned about preserving the independence of the judiciary, for there was no small measure of fear of judges armed with unbridled discretion. A bill was introduced into Parliament in 1674 to confirm judges' tenure and to assure them of a salary, but the opposition to unaccountable judges was so strong that the measure was defeated. Parliament subsequently dismissed four judges in April 1679, and the king dismissed a judge of Common Pleas and another of the King's Bench the following year. Chief Justice Sir William Scroggs was charged by Parliament with a variety of abuses of power, including discharging a grand jury before it completed its presentation, illegally refusing bail, and issuing blank general warrants. The king refused the dismissal, however, and quietly pensioned off the judge once the furor had subsided. Baron Weston and Sir Thomas Jones of the King's Bench were also impeached, but the latter was not removed.[22]

James II, who succeeded Charles II in 1685, resorted to the earlier tactic of canvassing the judges' opinions prior to taking an action. When some did not agree with his proposal on the dispensing power, James II dismissed two, Sir William Gregory and Sir Cresswell Levinz. His purge then extended to the chief justice of the Common Pleas, Sir Thomas Jones, and the chief baron of Exchequer, Sir William Montague, along with two others. Disagreements between judges and the monarch on the fate of a deserter led to the dismissal of two and the transfer of a third. When seven bishops were acquitted of charges of seditious libel in 1688 for objecting to James's second Declaration of Indulgence, the two judges involved, Sir Richard Holloway and Sir John Powell, were both dismissed. James II's use of his power of dismissal was effective, but the stance of a number of judges in opposition to him demonstrated that there did exist some judges whose allegiance was to the law.[23] The Crown's abuse of authority and the signs of resilient judicial independence were essential precursors to changes that were to follow James's abdication later in 1688.

Quamdiu se Bene Gesserint

The Glorious Revolution of 1688, that placed William III and Mary on the throne of England, marked the beginning of a new era for judicial independence and judicial accountability in England. The shift from the arbitrariness of Stuart monarchs to the new guarantee of tenure during good behavior evolved in stages over most of the following century. William and Mary assumed the throne jointly, but Mary's death in 1694 left William alone as the ruling monarch. Their practice from 1689 to 1702 was that judges held their positions according to good behavior, quamdiu se bene gesserint, but there was no statute prescribing the rule.[24] The Act of Settlement of 1700 and 1701 fixed judges' salaries and made their commissions contingent on their good behavior. The statutes also provided that judges could be removed by address of both houses of Parliament.[25]

The death of William III in 1702 raised the question of the extension of a judge's term beyond the life of the monarch who had appointed him. Chief Justice Holt and other judges who were in London met to discuss the issue and decided that their patents in office were terminated by the death of the king. Queen Anne, however, reappointed all but two of those sitting under her predecessor. The same question arose upon her death in 1714, but the conclusion was that the situation had already been resolved. Three judges' commissions were not renewed. Similarly, at the end of the reign of George I, one judge was not reappointed.[26] Near the end of his reign, the lord chancellor (both an executive and a judicial position) was impeached by the Commons and convicted by the Lords for having sold offices of masters in Chancery. He was sentenced to the Tower and fined 50,000 pounds.[27]

The point was definitively settled early in the reign of George III. The king addressed Parliament on March 3, 1761, saying: "I look upon the independence and uprightness of the Judges of the land as essential to the impartial administration of justice, as one of the best securities to the rights and liberties of my loving subjects and as most conducive to the honor of the crown; and I come now to recommend . . . that such farther provision may be made, for securing the Judges in the enjoyment of their office during their good behavior, not withstanding any such demise, as shall be most expedient".[28]

George III further requested that Parliament allow him to establish judges' salaries and to secure them through the length of their tenure.[29] Commons acted promptly to create and enact legislation to that effect, and, at least with respect to higher court judges, only minor changes have subsequently been made to their tenure in England and Wales. No other judge has been subject to impeachment by Parliament, and indeed the last impeachment of any kind, that of Lord of Melville, occurred in 1805. The alternative of a bill of attainder against judges was also rendered moot by the Forfeiture Act of 1870.[30]

Removal by the Crown on address of both houses of Parliament was the sole method that remained for dismissing a misbehaving judge from the bench. Only one, an Irish judge, Sir Jonah Barrington, who was accused of embezzlement of funds paid to the court, has been so removed.[31] Throughout the nineteenth century the primary attention paid to the courts was related to rationalizing their organization. Justices of the peace and county courts were organized between 1846 and 1849 to provide an inexpensive and speedy system of local courts. Education and qualifications for solicitors were also regularized during this time, and degrees in law were adopted by Cambridge and Oxford.[32] The Judicature Acts of 1873–75 prescribed reforms and reorganization of the higher courts, provided for a civil appeal to the Court of Appeal, and created the new High Court of Justice.[33] Most judges, unlike their predecessors under the Stuarts, tended to behave apolitically and accepted a declaratory, almost anti-intellectual, mechanistic approach to the law.[34]

The guarantee of tenure during good behavior for superior court judges was repeated in the Judicature Act of 1876, and address by Parliament was reaffirmed as the sole means of removal.[35] The motives that may prompt Parliament to seek removal of judges, however, were not stated and even today remain unclear. Moral delinquency as a reason for removal was cited by Cecil, who contends that the term does not encompass gross bad manners or unendurable interruptions.[36] Margaret Brazier argues that address by both houses of Parliament may occur for proven misbehavior or for "any reason satisfactory to Parliament" and asserts that this is currently the most common view.[37] The sole case of removal leaves prediction of the grounds for parliamentary address largely subject to speculation. A clear differentiation on accountability of judges exists between those on superior courts and on lower ones. That distinction has been recognized since the eighteenth century, as noted by Blackstone: "in order to maintain both the dignity and independence of the judges in the superior courts," tenure is for good behavior unless removed through address by Parliament.[38] Only the higher court judges—those on the High Court, Court of Appeal, and Law Lords—are governed by this guarantee, according to the Judicature Act of 1876. There is a single exception: the lord chancellor, who also holds cabinet status and is removable by the prime minister.[39] The overwhelming majority of judges are not on superior courts: approximately 97 percent are circuit court judges, magistrates (both stipendiary and lay), and recorders. These judges, who try criminal cases and hear smaller civil disputes,[40] may be removed, under the Court Act of 1971, by the lord chancellor for incapacity or misbehavior. Recorders serve for fixed terms that may not be renewed, and lay magistrates can be dismissed by the lord chancellor without specifying any grounds. A magistrate in 1985 sought judicial review of the lord chancellor's decision to dismiss her for having participated in a nuclear disarmament demonstration outside the building where she held court. That review was declined, even though an 1852 precedent existed for judicial review in the removal of a county court judge.[41]

Removal of judges on address of both houses of Parliament has been attempted 17 times but, as noted earlier, has succeeded only once in more than 200 years. The nature of the charges brought covers a broad field and fails to clarify the precise types of misbehavior that would make a judge removable.[42] In fact, in some instances in which there were parliamentary inquiries into the behavior of judges, it is only conjecture that the intent was to seek address. Parliamentary censure may have been the intended outcome.

Sir Francis Page, a baron of the Exchequer, was charged in 1722 with attempting to corrupt elections in the Borough of Banbury by offering a bribe and remission of a debt owed to him. The House of Commons heard witnesses and the argument of Baron Page's attorney. Though the debates were long, the charge was ultimately dismissed by a vote of 128 to 124. After a lapse of some decades, in 1805 another case was raised against a judge of Common Pleas in Ireland, Luke Fox. Whereas the accusations against Page had been heard in the Commons, the three petitions alleging that Fox had introduced his political preferences into his court were brought before the House of Lords. He was charged not only with trying to persuade a grand jury on political grounds, but also with fining the high sheriff for tardiness and insulting a trial jury. Because impeachment remained an option for the discipline of an erring judge, the prime minister urged the Lords to abandon the case. His argument was that if the Lords acted first and then sent the case to the Commons, who might choose impeachment over address, the Lords would have prejudged the case. The inquiry was dropped, and Fox continued on the bench for eleven years.

Even though the outcome of the Fox case would suggest that cases of potential address for removal should commence in the House of Commons, charges were brought against the lord chief justice, Lord Ellenborough, in both chambers. The Lords considered in 1813 whether he should be disciplined for presenting a misinterpretation of a witness's testimony in an inquiry into the conduct of Princess Caroline. Three years later 13 charges of abuse and bias in the exercise of Lord Chief Justice Ellenborough's judicial powers in a criminal case were brought before the House of Commons. In both Ellenborough cases the charges were dismissed.

An Irish baron of the Exchequer, James McClelland, was charged in the House of Commons in 1819 for ordering soldiers to clear his courtroom and barring access to it, in addition to an allegedly unlawful refusal of a postponement and some other forms of misconduct. The Commons agreed that whatever McClelland's behavior, there was no evidence of corrupt motives; the actions in question were ones of procedure. The House of Commons therefore declined to interfere. Mr. Justice Best was charged before the House of Commons in 1821 for fining the defendant for contempt of court three times in a blasphemous libel case he tried. The fines he imposed had, however, been upheld on appeal. The Commons, by a vote of 64 to 37, rejected the charge against him. Another Irish judge, Standish O'Grady, chief baron of the Irish Court of Exchequer, was charged before the Commons in 1821 with increasing his fees and introducing new ones. Two select committees found the fee increases to violate both the laws and the constitution, and the House as a whole agreed. The government, however, objected on several grounds, most of them procedural: the judge had not been allowed to defend himself, nor were witnesses heard on his behalf, nor was it clear that increasing fees amounted to corruption. After two years, the fee question was rendered moot by the abolition of fees, and the House voted 38 to 16 to drop the proceedings.

An English magistrate who also served as a judge of Great Sessions in

Wales, William Kendrick, was charged in 1825 with various abuses of his powers, including suppressing a felony charge. In the role of a magistrate, his behavior would not normally have been a matter for Parliament, but if he were found to have misused that office, grounds might be found for removing him from the higher judgeship. The House held a hearing but decided not go further with the inquiry. The next year, however, another charge against Kendrick alleged that he had used his power of prosecution to obtain the house of a defendant that would revert to the Crown upon conviction. The charge further contended that he had tried to persuade the man to plead guilty with the promise of a lenient sentence. Kendrick withdrew the prosecution, and the House halted the inquiry. This case was regarded as having established the authority of Parliament to inquire into private as well as official actions of judges if they were notoriously improper.

Only four years later the Commons and the Lords both voted for removal of the Irish judge, Sir Jonah Barrington, mentioned previously. A select committee was appointed to inquire into the case, but the accused judge refused to appear. His lawyer asked the full House of Commons to hear the judge, but it refused since he had already declined to appear before the committee. It also concluded that the relevant evidence was documentary and as a result did not require a hearing; the vote was for Barrington's removal. The Commons asked that the judge be removed as being unfit and setting a bad example. The Lords repeated the entire process, including witnesses and an appearance by the judge and his counsel, and reached the same conclusion. The Crown complied and removed Barrington from his position as judge of the High Court of Admiralty in Ireland.

Over the next four decades six additional petitions for removal by address were introduced. None of them, nor the four that came in the next century, resulted in the removal of the accused judges. The allegations raised and the reasons offered for not seeking removal provide some insight into the factors influencing the Commons in dealing with alleged judicial misconduct. Sir William Smith, another Irish judge, baron of the Irish Exchequer, was charged with unusual courtroom methods that the Commons believed fell into the category of procedure, not corruption. The select committee that conducted the investigation recommended, and the House agreed to, abandoning the investigation of allegations that the judge held court until early morning hours, did not begin sessions until afternoon, and made some political comments in his charges to grand juries.

Lord Abinger, lord chief baron of the Exchequer, was accused in the

House of Commons for blatantly making scurrilous political comments in his court about defendants who participated in strikes and demonstrations for extension of the franchise. He called their cause antithetical to the very future of the monarchy and the aristocracy. Parliament voted overwhelmingly (228 to 73), however, not to pursue the investigation, because the judge had no corrupt intentions. Similarly, in 1856 the Commons declined to investigate the conduct of an appeals court judge, Justice Torrens, who had affirmed the original decision in a matrimonial case involving a needy woman in Ireland. The Commons recognized that the decision had been upheld by an even higher appellate court and found no corrupt motives. The judge's conduct was not, therefore, considered further.

Not long thereafter, in 1865, the lord chancellor, Lord Westbury, was censured by both houses of Parliament for lack of proper judgment in handing the forced retirement of a clerk who had allegedly embezzled funds. The charges against the lord chancellor extended also to his choice of a successor for the clerk; the House of Commons claimed that he had appointed his son to the office, but the Lords found that the position had gone to someone who had bribed the lord chancellor's son. The censure prompted Lord Westbury to resign immediately. This is an instance of censure, not address, since the prime minister, not Parliament, has the power to remove the lord chancellor.

Lord Chief Baron Sir Fitzroy Kelly was the last judge charged in Parliament in the nineteenth century, and the allegations against him were eventually withdrawn. The purportedly questionable conduct by Kelly as a judge had occurred more than three decades before it was questioned in the House of Lords, in 1867. The claim was that he had made false statements before a committee of the House of Commons that was investigating possible corruption in his handling of an election. The lord chancellor and other peers investigated the charges and found no evidence of misconduct on Kelly's part.

Sir William Grantham, a judge of the King's Bench, was investigated by the House of Commons on two occasions, first in 1906 and again in 1911. In the first instance Grantham was accused of highly partisan and biased handling of two trials involving contested election results. House debates on the matter soundly condemned Grantham's behavior, but because he had displayed no corrupt motive, address for his removal was precluded. Strong calls for his resignation went unheeded. Five years later Grantham defended himself against the charges in a speech to the bar at Liverpool that directly attacked the House of Commons for its earlier investigation of him. This new indiscretion was brought before the House of Commons in a question to Prime Minister Herbert Asquith. The prime minister remarked on the general condemnation that Grantham's speech had elicited from both the legal profession and the press. That, he suggested, was sufficient; the extraordinary step of removal by address was not required.

Sir Henry McCardle's conduct as a judge on the King's Bench was raised as a question to Prime Minister Ramsay MacDonald in 1924. At issue was McCardle's conduct of a libel trial relating to a General Dyer's ordering troops to fire into a mob in India. The general had been dismissed for that action, but McCardle's instructions to the jury in the libel case included his personal assertion that the general had acted reasonably and had been improperly punished. Prime Minister MacDonald, while noting the inappropriateness of McCardle's remarks, said that the words did not constitute the kind of moral delinquency required for removal through address by Parliament.

Almost 50 years passed before another petition for address was considered in the House of Commons. Sir John Donaldson, president of the Industrial Relations Court, was charged with political bias and partiality by a large contingent of Labour MPs in 1973. His court had sequestered a large sum of money held by a union's political fund when the union failed to comply with a court order. Donaldson defended his court's actions publicly, and the lord chancellor tried to secure Donaldson's position in another public speech, in which he pointed to the partisan affiliation of those attacking the judge. The lord chancellor's statements drew criticism in Commons, where it was charged that he had tried to influence unduly proceedings in the Commons. Through a series of procedural decisions by the speaker of the House of Commons, neither the condemnation of the lord chancellor's behavior nor that of Judge Donaldson was ever debated; both issues simply lapsed.

Despite their number, the cases of parliamentary inquiry into judicial behavior do not lead to unambiguous guidelines about the nature of removal through address. Some vague contours of a parliamentary policy may, nonetheless, be seen. There seems to be a requirement that cases commence in the House of Commons, based on the Fox case in 1805. Even so, Lord Ellenborough was charged in both houses in 1813, and Lord Chief Baron Kelly's conduct was considered by the Lords in 1867. Authorities seem to agree, however, that the rule or at least the preferable course is that address originate in the Commons.[43] Parliament has consistently refused to proceed with address if the matters under inquiry involve procedure or administration of the courts or if the action in question was upheld by a higher court on appeal. Parliament also seems willing to tolerate almost any type of judicial behavior, no matter how egregious, as long as there are no corrupt motives. Even the most undisguised partisanship or intemperate actions by a judge seem acceptable in the absence of corrupt motives. It was also established in the case of William Kendrick that Parliament does regard a judge's private actions as appropriate for scrutiny if they are notorious; it has never removed, or for that matter even investigated, a judge on the basis of unofficial behavior.

Perhaps the only incentive for Parliament to pursue an address for removal is lack of deference to the parliamentary procedures. The only removal of a judge by address of both houses of Parliament, that of Sir Jonah Barrington, originated with charges that were no more serious than the cases brought against others on the bench. After Barrington refused to appear before the Commons committee investigating his alleged embezzlement, he was barred from presenting his case before the Commons as a whole. He participated in his defense before the Lords, but the refusal of the Commons to hear him had apparently charted the course for his removal. In no case has one chamber petitioned for address and the other disagreed. Rather, both chambers appear ready to accept any outside event that will remove the controversy from their purview, as for example, the elimination of the system of fees in the 1821 O'Grady case.

Judge Kendrick resigned in 1826 after the allegations against him in the House ended. Resignation or voluntary retirements in advance of a parliamentary investigation could well be the route that many judges follow when their official conduct falls under suspicion. There is no way to ascertain reliably the number of judges who have chosen or been encouraged to bow out of office in advance of an inquiry. David Pannick cites the instances of three judges who retired when impeded by mental or physical disability. An 85-year-old Irish judge was so deaf that he could not competently preside in court, and a petition for address was brought to the House of Commons. Since his retirement was imminent, Commons took no action. In 1891 Sir James Fitzjames Stephen retired when his mental illness became apparent. A high court judge in the 1950s refused to retire even when his mental deficiencies were manifestly interfering with his ability to conduct court. The solution was to assign no more cases to him, whereupon he finally took his pension.[44] No doubt if the record were public, it would reveal that a fair number of judges who acted injudiciously or who were impaired took retirement to avoid the humiliation of a public hearing or under pressure from their fellow judges or the lord chancellor.

In 1981 Parliament finally made statutory provision for removal of disabled judges and for mandatory retirement of aged individuals on the bench. The Supreme Court Act of 1981 provided that all judges on the Court of Appeal and High Court who had taken office after December 17, 1959, were subject to mandatory retirement at age 75. Crown Court judges were to retire at age 72, although the lord chancellor could extend that limit to 75 "as he thinks fit."[45] The retirement age for Crown Court judges was further lowered by statute in 1990 to 62, with provision for extension to 65 by the lord chancellor.[46] A process for removal of superior court judges who are incapable of performing their duties was also specified in the 1981 act. If, supported by a medical certificate, the lord chancellor finds that a judge is incapable of fulfilling court duties or resigning the office, the lord chancellor may declare the office vacant. That amounts to mandatory resignation. The lord chancellor, though, is required to gain the concurrence of specific other senior judges in making the determination of infirmity.[47]

Lower Court Judges

The Settlement Act of 1701 and the succeeding legislation discussed so far relate only to that tiny fraction of English and Welsh who comprise the Supreme Court—Court of Appeal, High Court of Justice, and the Crown Court. Circuit judges, recorders, assistant recorders, and magistrates, both stipendiary and lay, comprise the far larger proportion of judges sitting in England and Wales. The Courts Act of 1971 provided that circuit judges and recorders can be removed by the lord chancellor for incapacity or misbehavior, and recorders may be terminated also for failure to be available as required by their terms of appointment. Justices of the peace may be removed by the lord chancellor "as he sees fit," but removal has required a showing of good cause or grounds of infirmity or neglect.[48] Recorders, who serve for three-year terms, are often not reappointed because the lord chancellor finds their continuance undesirable. Between 1981 and 1986, for example, 27 were not renewed. The dismissals of circuit court judges or magistrates may be ascertained only by careful reading of parliamentary debates, where either an oral or written question may on occasion reveal an action by the lord chancellor. For example, a circuit court judge at Old Bailey in London who was dismissed in 1983 had been found guilty and fined on charges of smuggling whiskey and cigarettes.[49] As mentioned earlier, a magistrate was dismissed in 1985 for her participation in a nuclear disarmament demonstration outside the building in which she held court.[50] No formal hearing is required for dismissal, but the lord chancellor's prerogative appears not to be abused nor often used. Other lower court judges, whose positions fall under the jurisdiction of various officials, can be similarly removed. A Jersey bailiff, V. A. Tomes, with "a history of delay in delivery of his judicial judgments" was dismissed by privy counsellor with responsibility for Jersey. The bailiff had refused to resign.[51]

Judicial Immunity

Judicial independence in England and Wales also extends to immunity from civil liability for official actions, although there is a distinction drawn between higher and lower court judges. This protection is generally viewed as essential if judges are to administer justice freely. To do so, judges "must be protected against vexatious actions [and] should not be forever at risk of calumny for slight errors."[52] The safeguard is usually traced to the early seventeenth century, also the period when the status of inferior and superior court judges was first differentiated. The earliest case involved lower court judges in the 1612 *Marshalsea Case*. The Marshalsea Court, that had jurisdiction only in matters concerning the royal household, acted in a case involving two individuals who did not fall under that jurisdiction. Since the court had no jurisdiction to hear the case, the judges were liable to pay damages.[53]

In the *Marshalsea Case,* a higher court set the bounds for an inferior one, but the superior court judges did not apply the same rule to their own. The controlling case for superior court judges originated in the Court of Oyer and Terminer at the Old Bailey, in which a juryman was imprisoned improperly for refusing to follow the judge's order to convict the Quaker defendants. The juryman sued for damages for false imprisonment, citing the *Marshalsea Case.* The Court of Common Pleas, however, held that "though [the judges] were mistaken, yet they *acted judicially,* and for that reason no action will lie against the defendant [emphasis mine]."[54] One exception to the absolute immunity of upper court judges was made in the Habeas Corpus Act of 1679, which reiterated a judge's protection against liability for any judicial action or omission except refusal to issue a writ of habeas corpus while on vacation.[55]

A series of cases during the nineteenth century reaffirmed the shield against civil liability for superior court judges, but the protection of inferior judges was less clear. The Crown Proceedings Act of 1947 did not illuminate the point; that law was designed to define the liability of the Crown and stated that in tort questions, the Crown is "not in any circumstances liable for wrongs committed by 'judicial officers,' that is judges or members of tribunals."[56] The liabilities of both tiers of judges were merged, albeit for only a brief time, in the decision by the Court of Appeal in *Sirros v. Moore* in 1974.

Michael Sirros, a Turkish alien who had overstayed the limits of his visa, was brought before a magistrate, who fined him and ordered his deportation. Sirros appealed to the Divisional Court, where Judge Moore dismissed the appeal. For reasons that remain obscure, Moore ordered Sirros held after the defendant had left the courtroom. After a day and a half in jail, Sirros was granted bail. He then filed a suit against the judge and the police officers, alleging assault and false imprisonment. Judge Moore had dismissed Sirro's appeal on the erroneous assumption that he had no jurisdiction in the case, when in fact he did. Could Sirros in these circumstances win damages from the judge? Master of the Rolls, Lord Denning, with the general concurrence of Lords Ormrod and Buckley, decided that Judge Moore was protected from civil liability. Denning further asserted that, "no matter that the judge was under some gross error or ignorance, or was actuated by envy, hatred and malice and all uncharitableness, he is not liable to an action."[57] The crucial factor was whether or not the judge was acting within his jurisdiction or at least believed that he was doing so. Denning argued, moreover, that if the judge had acted in a criminal fashion by accepting bribes or other forms of corruption, he could be liable in criminal courts. Lord Denning then extended the rule by asserting that "as matter of principle the judges of superior courts have no greater claim to immunity than the judges of the lower courts."[58] Both Lords Buckley and Ormrod agreed in this instance with extending the protection against civil liability.

Parliament did not, however, accept the broad statement of law offered by the Court of Appeal. The Justice of the Peace Act of 1979 specified that magistrates had no immunity if they acted outside their powers, or even within their authority when malice or special damage could be proven. Actions outside their jurisdiction, if reasonable and taken in good faith, could be indemnified from public funds. To limit frivolous claims under the law, Parliament also provided that damages were restricted to a single penny, even if the magistrate exceeded his powers, as long as the plaintiff was guilty of the offense and not excessively punished. The House of Lords in the 1985 case of *McC v. Mullan* concurred that justices of the peace could be civilly liable if they had acted beyond their jurisdiction.[59] That decision also questioned the absence of distinction between superior and inferior court judges, leaving the status of lower court judges, who are not magistrates, quite unsettled.

Future and Reform of the System

Criticism of those who staff the bench in England and Wales has been considerable, not only in recent years. Boswell quotes Dr. Samuel Johnson as saying in 1775: "There is no reason why a Judge should hold his office for life, more than any other person in public trust. A Judge may be partial otherwise than to the Crown: we have seen Judges partial to the populace. A Judge may become corrupt, and yet there may not be legal evidence against him. . . . A Judge may grow unfit for his office in many ways."[60] Charles Dickens's *Bleak House,* published in 1853, constituted a resounding condemnation of the English bench and bar.

Indictments this century are more focused on a single alleged form of bias in the system: "there is a certain lack of touch with the common man and in consequence absence of appreciation of the many problems he faces."[61] Lord Justice Scutton commented in 1923 on the problems that attend leaving matters of justice to a small, privileged social elite: "It is very difficult sometimes to be sure that you have put yourself into a thoroughly impartial position between two disputants, one of your own class and one not of your own class."[62] The criticism, then, as Brazier put it, is the equation of judicial independence with preservation of the status quo.[63]

Griffith notes the dominance on the bench of the upper and upper-middle classes from 1820 to 1968 and links this disproportionate representation of the larger population to the requirement that superior court judges be chosen from the among the ranks of barristers: "to become a successful barrister . . . it is necessary to have financial support and so the background has to be that of the reasonably well-to-do family."[64] That connection has also been empirically demonstrated. Though family status does not directly explain the path to upper courts, it does play an indirect role.[65]

There is, moreover, an overwhelming dominance of white men on all of the English benches. In October of 1990, of the 83 High Court judges, only two were women. Similar disparities are reflected down the judicial ladder: 422 county court judges, of whom 18 were women; 422 circuit court judges, of whom 18 were women; 742 recorders, of whom 18 were women; and 380 assistant recorders, of whom 21 were women.[66] By 1992, more women were present on the bench, but not a large proportion. For example, one additional woman judge joined the ranks of the High Court, and the ratio of county court judges was 447 men to 22 women.[67] More telling, however, may be the fact that until autumn of 1991, no records were kept on the ethnic origins of the judiciary. It was believed, however, that in 1992, of 266 district judges, there "are at present no black district judges" and "there is one Asian—who is a woman—and 18 women holding that office."[68]

The controversies that seem to be enveloping the English bench reflect that lack of heterogeneity. Comments offered by judges from the bench reflect insensitivity, if not blatant sexism and racism. Judge Starforth Hill, in sentencing an 18-year-old youth who admitted attempting to have sex with an eight-year-old girl, remarked that "she was not entirely an angel herself." Another judge, when giving a man a suspended sentence for strangling his wife because of her nagging, said that he had borne the nagging better than most people might. Or, in a last example from press reports, a judge gave a man a two-year probationary sentence for sexually abusing his stepdaughter during his wife's pregnancy and explained his decision with a comment on the wife's lack of sexual appetite that created problems "for a healthy young husband."[69]

The need to reform the system, at least that for naming judges, has received some official attention in recent years. The lord chancellor's Office issued a report in 1986 that explained, if only in the broadest generalities, the process used for selecting superior court judges.[70] The next year a procedure was announced to allow grievances to be filed against judges. The Courts and Legal Services Act of 1990 somewhat lessened the statutory requirements to serve on the higher courts, with the intention of widening the pool of eligible candidates. The previous qualification for lord justices of the Court of Appeal had been 15 years' experience as a barrister or service as a High Court judge; that for a puisne, or superior court judge, had been ten years of experience as a barrister. The requirement for both was lowered to 10 years of High Court qualification or, in the case of High Court judgeships, two years as a circuit court judge.[71]

The current system for disciplining judges, which has existed virtually since 1761, does not rely only on the formal mechanism of address by both houses of Parliament. It also assumes that checks on judicial behavior exist in the form of the press, the Court of Appeal and lord chancellor, and the pressure of senior judges.[72] Those informal means of policing and curbing the behavior of erring judges have not been adequate in the view of the opposition Labour and Liberal Democrat parties, both of whom have proffered proposals for changes. The Liberal Democrats would establish a Judicial Service Commission to nominate all senior judges. Labour suggests creation of an independent commission to name judges. Neither of these proposed reforms would, however, affect the removal or discipline of a sitting judge. Brazier proposes more far-reaching changes that would include a Judicial Service Commission and Circuit Judicial Committees. These would be staffed by sitting judges on the higher courts but would also include some lay members to "offset professional insularity and . . . to ensure that the case was argued for further widening the pool of potential judicial candidates."[73] His vision of the scope of the commission's work would include receiving, investigating, and resolving complaints against sitting judges. He would leave in place the machinery for address by Parliament to remove judges who were not persuaded to resign or retire by ongoing investigations against them or by criticism from the commission.[74]

Change has come gradually to legal systems in general and especially to the English one. The existing system for supervising judicial behavior evolved over several centuries, and only minor adjustments to it have been made in more than 300 years. Address by Parliament may no longer be the most feasible method for ridding the bench of an unethical judge, given the press of other legislative business. Indeed, there have been no serious attempts to use that process in more than 20 years. Though criticism of the existing system seems to be mounting, similar negative critiques have been made before. None have resulted in more than a bit of tinkering with the system. Changes are more likely to be made in how judges are recruited to the bench than in ways to remove them, once there. The underlying assumption is that if superior individuals, representing a larger slice of the population, are named to the bench, they should reduce the need for discipline or removal at a later time. The basic structure governing judicial ethics and tenure that has matured and evolved incrementally over the centuries is not likely to undergo any significant reformation in the near future.

Chapter 5

The United States

The approach to judicial accountability in the United States is emblematic of the British heritage. At least at the national level the emphasis is on judicial independence, and accountability is clearly secondary. The 13 original states initially relied on their experiences as British colonies, but over time and with national expansion the states have experimented widely with alternative ways of judging the judges. The 50 states have acted autonomously and creatively to fashion an array of mechanisms and have served as political laboratories for testing diverse systems. When one appears viable, it is typically adopted and modified by sister states. Disparate ideological, practical, and historical themes are reflected in the kaleidoscopic variations among systems for selecting, removing, and disciplining judges across the American states.

The national scheme that governs roughly a thousand U.S. judges, from trial courts to the Supreme Court, borrows clearly from the English model. Judges are appointed by the president, with the advice and consent of the Senate, and serve for life or good behavior. Even the now abandoned English process of impeachment is preserved as the sole means of removing a judge from office. Dissatisfaction with that device led, however, to the evolution during the twentieth century of an auxiliary mechanism that can be used to monitor the conduct of erring judges when their alleged offenses fall short of what is impeachable and also to motivate congressional action when impeachment may indeed be warranted.

The states, on the other hand, have adopted various means for ensuring the accountability of their judges. The era of Jacksonian democracy introduced the notion of naming and removing judges through elections; Mississippi altered its constitution in 1832 to provide for partisan elections for all judges and thus began a trend that continues to the present. By the Progressive era, judges were viewed as little more than hack politicians.[1] As a consequence, reform movements flourished, and nonpartisan elections gained in popularity. In 1992, 37 states used either partisan or nonpartisan elections to recruit and to remove judges on at least one level of courts. The other innovation that grew out of the call for reform was the merit selection/merit retention system, whereby candidates for judgeships are screened and a limited list of "qualified" candidates from which judges must be selected is provided to an appointing authority. The appointer, usually the governor or the state legislature, makes the final selection. At some future time, the newly appointed judge is made accountable to the electorate through a retention election in which judges run, without opposition, on their records. In other words, a semblance of democratic accountability is preserved. This approach is used by 22 states for at least one level of judgeship.[2] Twelve states simply appoint some of their judges for a fixed term.[3]

The states have also adopted a variety of other means for removing judges. Almost all provide for impeachment or executive removal upon address of the legislature, and a few permit the voters to unseat undesirable jurists through recall elections. That none of these schemes has been wholly satisfactory is clear, and now all 50 states and the District of Columbia have adopted supplementary judicial conduct organizations. These bodies, typically composed of both legal and lay representatives and judges, receive, investigate, and make recommendations on complaints of judicial misconduct. Creativity in how to make judges accountable for their behavior has typified state approaches.

U.S. judges, both state and federal, have been granted protection from civil liability in the course of their official duties even if they act in excess of their jurisdictions.[4] More recently, however, a small exception to that blanket immunity has been carved out in a very narrow category of civil rights cases involving requests for injunctive relief.[5]

Impeachment of Federal Judges

The U.S. Constitution, written in 1787, includes several provisions relating to the appointment and tenure of federal judges. Article 3 states, in a paraphrase of the English statute, that judges "shall hold their Offices during good Behavior, and shall, at stated Times, receive for their Services, a Compensation, which shall not be diminished during their Continuance in Office." Article 2, section 2, provides that they shall be nominated by the president, with the advice and consent of the Senate. Article 2, section 4, also says that "the President, Vice President and all Civil Officers of the United States, shall be removed from Office on Impeachment for and Conviction of Treason, Bribery or other high Crimes and Misdemeanors." Article 1 specifies that the House of Representatives, like its English counterpart, can bring charges by a majority vote, and that the Senate alone may try and convict, by two-thirds majority. Departing from the English antecedent, punishment is limited by that article to removal from office.

Discipline and removal of judges gained scant attention at the Constitutional Convention in 1787. The English good behavior standard was later defended in the ratification discussions as "the best expedient which can be devised in any government to secure a steady, upright and impartial administration of the laws;"[6] permanency in office was argued to be "the citadel of the public justice and the public security."[7] At the Constitutional Convention, debates on impeachment centered on its potential use as a check on the executive. Alexander Hamilton, however, subsequently stated unambiguously that impeachment was likewise applicable to judges and was the only measure "consistent with the necessary independence of the judicial character."[8]

The impeachment mechanism has been little used in the more than 200 years since its introduction in the United States, and contrary to the expectations of the framers, it has rarely been used against executive officials. Senator William Blount (1798), President Andrew Johnson (1868), and Secretary of War William Belknap (1876) are the only nonjudicial officials against whom impeachments were voted by the House of Representatives. None of the three was convicted by the requisite two-thirds of the Senate. The primary targets of impeachment have instead been federal judges—13 of whom were impeached by the House and seven convicted by the Senate. Hundreds of other impeachment resolutions have been introduced in the House of Representatives, and U.S. judges were the targets in the overwhelming majority of the cases. More than 60 allegations against judges were treated by the House as sufficiently serious to merit investigations.

Hamilton had declared that impeachable offenses were political in nature, "as they relate chiefly in injuries done immediately to the society itself."[9] Indeed, the earliest instances of investigations and impeachments of federal judges can appropriately be labeled "political," at least to the extent that partisan lines in voting were clearly distinguishable. Political events during the first judicial impeachment make clear the partisan nature of the process. The Federalist Party was literally swept from both the presidency and a majority of Congress in the elections of 1800, and the lame duck Federalist Congress made a futile attempt to salvage some role in the national government by passing the Judiciary Act of 1801. That law was designed, among other things, to deprive newly elected President Thomas Jefferson of making a Supreme Court appointment. The law provided for the permanent reduction of the number of justices on the highest court from six to five upon the retirement or resignation of a sitting justice. The Jeffersonians, upon taking office in March, retaliated by canceling the 1802 term of the Federalist-dominated Supreme Court and thereafter repealing the 1801 Judiciary Act. Pursuing their attack on the Federalist judiciary, Jefferson and his lieutenants contemplated impeachment as a means for controlling and removing offensive Federalist judges from the bench,[10] and in 1804 Federalist Judge John Pickering of New Hampshire was impeached by the House of Representatives.

U.S. Judge Pickering has the dubious distinction of being the first person impeached and convicted in the United States. He had written the New Hampshire constitution and as a revolutionary patriot had cemented his reputation as an outstanding citizen.[11] After being appointed chief justice of the New Hampshire courts in 1791, he had developed a nervous disorder that interfered with his ability to serve on the bench. The New Hampshire legislature attempted to remove him, an action that failed by one vote. Fellow Federalists in New Hampshire sought to solve Pickering's difficulties by obtaining a federal judicial appointment for him. They succeeded, and he served competently for a while, but his condition worsened into a combination of mental derangement and alcoholism.[12] The Judiciary Act of 1801, in creating a new circuit court judgeship, relieved Pickering of his duties, but repeal of that law returned him to the bench. At the opening day of the trial of *U.S. v. Eliza,* he cursed from the bench and even attempted to cane a lawyer. He could no longer serve, but his insanity prevented him from resigning, and the absence of pensions for civil servants kept his family from acting.[13]

Pickering was charged before the House of Representatives with "high crimes and misdemeanors" in four articles, three of which were tied to his behavior in the trial of *Eliza* and another to his "loose morals and intemperate habits," "total intoxication," and "evil example."[14] Aaron Burr, as vice president, conducted the whole affair before the Senate with elaborate

ceremony and "like most Americans . . . looked to England for precedents."[15] Eleven days were devoted to debate over trivial details before the
Senate dispatched its sergeant at arms to New Hampshire with a summons
for Pickering to appear five weeks later. Pickering did not appear; instead
Robert Goodloe Harper, counsel, pleaded the case: "feebleness of body and
mind, his poverty, the inclement season."[16] Eight days of testimony were
taken by seven Jeffersonian Republicans before the Senate, and when they
had finished the Senate convicted Pickering by a vote of 19 to 7 on all four
articles. Seven senators refused to vote, but those who did split along
strictly partisan lines.[17] Almost simultaneously, Jeffersonians in the House
voted to impeach Supreme Court Justice Samuel Chase.

The impeachment of Chase, who was by any standard a flamboyant and
controversial figure, has generated considerable debate. Most commentators conclude that he should not have been impeached, and indeed he was
not convicted by the Senate. William Rehnquist, himself a chief justice of
the Supreme Court, in 1992 described Chase's acquittal as a victory for separation of powers and the independence of the judiciary.[18] Berger, however, reached the opposite conclusion, on the basis that Chase was clearly
a biased judge.[19] Chase had been a signer of the Declaration of Independence and had served in the Continental Congress until forced to leave under a cloud. He opposed the Constitution, and in the Maryland ratifying
conventions argued that Congress under the proposed constitution would
represent wealthy merchants and not the people. He entered business but
was forced to petition for bankruptcy. Beginning his judicial career in 1788,
he was chief judge of the General Court of Maryland by 1791, but his conduct caused the Maryland Assembly to seek his removal. A simple majority voted against him but not the necessary two-thirds to force him from
the bench. Chase was proposed to President George Washington for the
Supreme Court by Secretary of War James McHenry, who claimed that the
judge's past errors were more than overcome by his many talents. He was
nominated as an associate justice to the U.S. Supreme Court on January 26,
1796, and the next day the Senate confirmed him without opposition.[20]

Chase's comportment as a Supreme Court justice gave rise to no complaints, and he was the author of some major decisions that have been characterized as having a "colorful quality," that together with their "positive-
ness of expression [and] their richness in 'political science' . . . , contributed
to give his opinions predominant importance in this period."[21] Chase
nonetheless sought controversy by actively campaigning for John Adams's
reelection in 1800 and by lobbying for passage of the Alien and Sedition

Acts. His conduct while riding circuit, moreover, drew no small measure of criticism. He often acted not as the judge but as a prosecutor in attempts to secure convictions of Republicans charged under the Alien and Sedition laws. For example, in the trials of John Fries in Pennsylvania and James Thomas Callender in Virginia, he was overtly partisan. In Fries's trial, only jurors indicating a bias against the defendant were permitted on the jury, and Fries was not represented by counsel. He was convicted and sentenced to death by Chase, but President Adams commuted the penalty. Chase, when presiding over the Callender case, refused to permit the defendant's lawyers to address the possible unconstitutionality of the Sedition law, and his conduct of the trial was described as intemperate, dogmatic, and high-handed.[22] Even more damning, his charge in 1803 to a Baltimore grand jury was viewed by Jefferson and his allies as beyond any bounds of acceptable judicial behavior. Chase, in that circumstance, attacked the repeal of the Judiciary Act of 1801 and the Maryland constitutional revision that permitted universal male suffrage, which would, according to Chase, sink "our republican constitution . . . into mobocracy."[23]

President Jefferson, taking note of Chase's remarks, wrote to his leading partisan in the House of Representatives: "Ought this seditious and official attack on the principles of our Constitution and on the proceedings of a State go unpunished?"[24] Jefferson's complicity in the subsequent impeachment proceedings was always in the background. He tried to woo Aaron Burr, whose cooperation seemed important since he would preside over the Senate proceedings and who was also seen as vulnerable because of his indictment in New Jersey for killing Alexander Hamilton in a duel in 1804.[25] Burr was, by most accounts, unmoved and generally conducted a fair hearing for Chase before the Senate.[26]

Eight articles of impeachment against Chase were voted by the House and presented to the Senate. The first related to the trial of John Fries, five others addressed Chase's conduct of the Callender case, and the last two involved grand juries, one in Delaware and one in Baltimore.[27] Preliminaries of the Senate trial began in late November 1804, but the actual trial itself did not begin until January 2, 1805. Chase at that time requested a delay until March, but the House managers (John Randolph, William Giles, and Joseph Nicholson) demanded that it start immediately. The date was finally moved to February 4. On that day Chase, accompanied by four attorneys, appeared to answer the charges in a 78-page statement that took three and a half hours to read. When the trial resumed on February 9, John Randolph responded, but his ringing rhetoric fell flat beside the cold legal logic presented by Chase.[28] Over the next 9 days, 18 prosecution witnesses and 31 for the defense testified, plus 5 prosecution rebuttal witnesses. The summation speeches for both sides took another eight days; on March 1, 1805, the trial ended, and a vote was taken on each of the articles of impeachment. The Republicans, with 25 senators, might have expected to convict easily, but unlike their voting in the Pickering case, they broke ranks and the necessary two-thirds majority to convict (23 votes) was not forthcoming on any charge. In fact, on one count, the vote was unanimous for acquittal, and on none was the vote stronger than 19 to 15 for conviction.[29] Chase was acquitted on all charges.

The Chase trial had a number of consequences. Federal judges were said to "improve remarkably" and thereafter refrained from participation in partisan politics.[30] They seemed to have embraced voluntarily a rule akin to the French obligation of political reserve. Randolph, convinced of the inefficacy of impeachment, introduced a constitutional amendment to make all federal judges removable by the president upon address of both houses of Congress; that proposal, like all subsequent ones, failed. Jefferson, who had once viewed impeachment as "the most formidable weapon for the purposes of a dominant faction," came to regard the process as "a mere scarecrow," a "farce."[31] Chase returned to the Supreme Court though he was often ill with gout, and he served there until his death in 1811 at the age of 71.[32]

The Chase trial seems also to have buried impeachment as a political weapon for more than a generation. Overtly partisan concerns were not to color judicial impeachments again soon, though some of the underlying motives of several later proceedings may well have been partisan. Impeachment was not forgotten, however, and James Peck of the U.S. District Court in Missouri was impeached by the House in 1830 by a vote of 123 to 49. The sole article related to Peck's use of the contempt power to imprison Luke Edward Lawless for publishing an 18-point letter to the editor in the *Missouri Advocate and St. Louis Enquirer* that criticized Peck's decision in a land grant case.[33] Peck's quite elaborate response to the Senate was that the letter by Lawless misrepresented his opinion; moreover, there were other, undecided land claims in which Lawless represented litigants. Ten witnesses were presented by the House managers and 10 by Peck, along with depositions and other physical evidence. The trial, which had begun May 1830, resumed in December of that year, and concluded on January 31, 1831, with a Senate vote of 21 guilty to 22 not guilty, with two abstentions.[34]

West H. Humphreys, a federal district judge in Tennessee, was impeached in 1862 on a voice vote for seven counts of supporting secession and holding office in the Confederacy. The case against Humphreys was relatively straightforward, since he had openly supported Tennessee's secession from the Union and was, at the time of his impeachment, serving as a judge for the Confederate States of America and trying defendants in Tennessee who were loyal to the Union.[35] Legal niceties were maintained and all formalities preserved as five House managers were named to prosecute the case before the Senate. When Humphreys could not be physically located by the Senate sergeant at arms who went to Tennessee to serve the summons, the trial proceeded with neither Humphreys nor a counsel for him. Five witnesses were summoned and Humphreys was found guilty by all senators on two articles and acquitted on one; at least one senator voted not guilty on each of the remaining four articles.[36]

Partisanship did not seem to be a factor in either the Peck or the Humphreys case. For the remainder of the nineteenth century, no more judges were impeached. Federal judges, when investigations began to center on them, developed a new strategy: they resigned rather than face impeachment. Indeed, since 1818 a total of 22 judges have followed that path when allegations of misconduct against them began.[37] Thomas Irwin resigned in 1859, as did Mark Delahay and Charles T. Sherman in 1873, and Edward Durrell and Richard Busteed in 1875.[38] Another spate of congressional inquiries into the conduct of federal judges ensued at the beginning of the twentieth century, prompting eight additional resignations and five impeachments between 1903 and 1936.[39] Of those who were impeached, only two were convicted and one, George English, resigned before a Senate trial. This flurry of proceedings has been interpreted as a Democratic Party attempt to remove Republican judges and to embarrass the dominant Republicans or, in some cases, as more narrowly drawn political games.[40]

Twelve articles of impeachment were voted against District Court Judge Charles Swayne of the Northern District of Florida by a voice vote in the House in December 1904. The charges, supported by a joint resolution of the Florida state legislature, alleged that Swayne had used a private railway car belonging to a railroad company in receivership, along with other irregularities in bankruptcy proceedings, abuse of the contempt power, claiming expenses to which he was not entitled, and not living in his district. In the Senate trial in 1905, multiple witnesses testified for each side, and on February 27 Swayne was acquitted on all charges.[41] The voting in the Senate, both on procedural matters and on all articles of impeachment, was characterized by almost solid bloc voting by the Democrats along the partisan voting lines on Swayne's confirmation in 1890.[42]

Commerce Court Judge Robert W. Archbald, also a Republican, was impeached by the House in 1912, but did not fare as well as Swayne had. The Justice Department had originally investigated Archbald's behavior but took no action. The House impeached Archibald, however, by a vote of 223 to 1, on 13 articles alleging that he had abused his judicial influence to further his personal business interests, had pressured litigants before his court for special considerations, and had solicited personal contributions from attorneys practicing in his court.[43] Archbald was convicted on five counts by a coalition of Democrats, Progressives, and Republicans linked to Theodore Roosevelt.[44]

A dozen years passed before the conduct of another judge claimed the attention of the House of Representatives. George W. English of Illinois was charged with flagrant abuse of his office, including shows of favoritism in appointing both receivers and attorneys and pressure on banks with whom he had ordered bankruptcy funds deposited for favorable loan conditions for himself. He was impeached with virtually no supporters by the House of Representatives in November 1926. English saved the Senate the task of a trial by resigning once the articles of impeachment were passed.[45]

Many in both the House and the Senate wished that Harold Louderback of California would follow the easy route of resignation after he was impeached by the House in 1933. He did not, however, and was rewarded with vindication in the Senate. Louderback had allegedly shown favoritism in appointing receivers and allowing them to charge excessive fees. One of those receivers was the son of the senator who had recommended Louderback's appointment to President Calvin Coolidge in 1928. The charges were suspect from the beginning. The House committee that had initially investigated the allegations had voted 17 to 5 against impeachment, but the full House passed the articles, 183 to 142, despite that negative recommendation.[46] A nine-day trial began in the Senate on May 15, and at its conclusion Louderback was acquitted on all charges. On only one article of impeachment was there even a simple majority voting for his guilt.[47]

Halsted Ritter, a U.S. district judge for southern Florida, was the last federal judge to be impeached during this era. The judge was impeached on seven articles for showing favoritism, irregularities in handling bankruptcy litigation, illegally accepting money from his former law partner, and evading income tax.[48] The Senate trial consumed every afternoon for 10 days in early April 1936, and the Senate's final verdict was a curious one.

Ritter was acquitted on the six articles that addressed specific unethical acts, but convicted by a bare two-thirds majority (56 to 28) on the last summary article: bringing his court "into scandal and disrepute, to the prejudice of said court, and public confidence in the administration of justice therein."[49]

Revival of Impeachment

No other judge faced impeachment for the next 50 years. Congressional investigations were authorized and impeachment resolutions were introduced, but none even reached the floor of the House of Representatives for a vote. District Judge Martin Manton was tried and convicted in 1939 on criminal charges, but dutifully resigned his office before his trial commenced. Former Illinois governor and incumbent U.S. Circuit Judge Otto Kerner was convicted in criminal court in 1973 of conspiracy to commit bribery and mail fraud, tax evasion, false statements to the Internal Revenue Service, and perjury. The offenses covered the time that he had been governor and extended into his tenure as a U.S. judge. Kerner had argued unsuccessfully that he should not be subject to a criminal trial, for conviction there would be tantamount to removal from office. Only the House and Senate, according to articles 1 and 2 of the Constitution, he claimed, could remove him, through impeachment. The criminal trial, in other words, would usurp the exclusive congressional prerogatives. That case was heard by the U.S. Court of Appeals for the Seventh Circuit, which held that Kerner's federal office did not bar criminal prosecutions, for "protection of tenure is not a license to commit crime or a forgiveness of crimes committed before taking office."[50] That court found that the separation of powers was no bar to criminal prosecution and even went so far as to state that because of the political overtones of impeachment, judicial independence was better protected in courts of law, where the "issues are heard in a calm and reasoned manner and are subject to the rules of evidence, the presumption of innocence and other safeguards."[51] Kerner resigned from his judgeship, and the House of Representatives chose not to pursue his impeachment.

During this time, there were a number of congressional inquiries into the behavior of federal judges, most notably Supreme Court Justices William O. Douglas and Abe Fortas. Though no impeachment proceedings were brought, Fortas eventually resigned from the Court in 1968, claiming that he had done nothing improper, "but in view of the outcry in the press, it would be in the best interest of the court for him to resign."[52] A new twist on the monitoring of judicial conduct emerged in the 1980s. The public integrity office of the U.S. Justice Department took the initiative in rooting out corrupt behavior. In rather quick succession, three U.S. district judges were indicted on criminal charges. The first trial of one ended in a hung jury, but the second trial brought a conviction. Another judge was also convicted, and the third was acquitted in a jury trial. None of the three followed the examples of Fortas, who resigned to spare the judiciary embarrassment, or Kerner, who resigned after his conviction.

In the first of the three cases, U.S. District Court Judge Harry Claiborne of Nevada was charged with two counts of conspiracy, one of obstruction of justice, one of wire fraud, three of making false statements on his income tax, and one of false statements on his government financial disclosure form. The prosecution's first attempt to convict him ended in a mistrial on April 7, 1984. The second trial was greatly pared down—the charges were solely two years of income tax evasion and false statements on the ethics in government form. Claiborne was found guilty on both charges of income tax evasion and sentenced to two years in prison and two fines of $5,000 each. Claiborne then did what no other federal judge had ever done: even though a convicted felon, he remained in office rather than resigning.[53]

The House of Representatives, by a unanimous vote of 406 to 0 on July 22, 1986, impeached Claiborne for underreporting his taxes in two years, for making false statements on his income taxes the same two years, and for bringing the federal courts into disrepute. In the first use of a Senate rule adopted in 1935, the Senate allowed an evidentiary committee to hear evidence and report to the full Senate on impeachment. The bipartisan evidentiary committee began seven days of hearings in September 1986. The following month the Senate, in lieu of a trial, heard one-hour presentations by the House managers and by Claiborne's defense. The next day the Senate found Claiborne guilty on three charges, two counts of income tax evasion and one of bringing the judiciary into disrepute.[54]

In the second case in the 1980s, Alcee L. Hastings, U.S. district judge in Florida, was charged with conspiracy to solicit and accept a bribe and with corruptly influencing and impeding the administration of justice in 1981. Because of a flurry of appeals that Hastings filed, his case did not go to trial until 1983, when a jury acquitted him of all charges. Hastings returned to the bench, but an investigation by his fellow judges began almost immediately. The Judicial Conduct and Disability Act of 1980, which will be discussed later, allowed for complaints to be filed and a judge to be investigated by a committee of other federal judges. Such a committee was formed to investigate a litany of allegations concerning Hastings's conduct, not only the original criminal charges but also allegations of illegal and unethical behavior in his criminal trial. In August 1986 the committee concluded that on several counts, including the original bribery allegation, Hastings's conduct "might constitute one or more grounds for impeachment." The committee's report was certified by the U.S. Judicial Conference and forwarded to the House of Representatives, where a resolution impeaching Hastings was filed on March 23, 1987.

The House committee that investigated the Hastings case did not begin its deliberations until May of the next year. After seven days of testimony, that committee unanimously forwarded 17 articles of impeachment to the full House, which concurred by a vote of 413 to 3. The Senate again used an evidentiary committee to gather evidence in June, and closing arguments by both sides were presented before the full Senate on October 19, 1989. The Senate then found Hastings guilty by the requisite two-thirds majority on all but three articles. Though removed from the federal judiciary, Hastings used his self-proclaimed negative celebrity status to win election to the U.S. House of Representatives in 1992.[55]

A third district court judge's criminal case was winding its way through investigation and trial while both Hastings and Claiborne were undergoing the impeachment process before Congress. Walter L. Nixon, serving in Mississippi, was charged with receiving an illegal gratuity and with three counts of committing perjury before a grand jury. An illegal gratuity is less direct than a bribe and involves a public official's accepting something of value with the expectation that at some undetermined future time there will be reciprocity in an official act. On February 8, 1986, Nixon was convicted on two counts of perjury, and the next month was sentenced to two concurrent five-year prison terms. Nixon, like Claiborne, refused to resign. Both claimed that their refusals were based on tainted prosecutions in their trials and targeting by the Justice Department. The precedent that a convicted felon could not continue to hold the office of judge had already been set by House and Senate actions in the Claiborne case. Even so, both chambers of Congress had to impeach, try, and convict Nixon formally if he were not to continue as a federal judge, even while serving a prison term. On May 10, 1989, the House unanimously impeached Nixon on two counts of perjury and a third count of bringing the courts into disrepute. The Senate, after hearings by an evidentiary committee, heard final arguments on November 1, 1989, and permitted senators to ask written questions of both the

House managers and the defense. Two days later, Nixon was convicted by overwhelming majorities on all three articles.[56]

While these three cases were before Congress, two other federal judges were also convicted in criminal cases. Judge Robert Aguilar of California was found guilty on five counts of conspiracy, obstruction of justice, and unlawful disclosure of wiretaps in 1990, and Judge Robert F. Collins of Louisiana was convicted on bribery charges in 1991. Collins resigned, and Aguilar's removal dragged on. The list of judges serving on the federal bench after criminal convictions was growing. Of course, the size of the federal judiciary was as well. In 1789 there were only 19 federal judges—6 on the Supreme Court and 13 district judges. Between 1956 and 1990, the number of federal judges almost tripled, with the 1990 authorization of additional judges bringing the totals to 9 justices of the Supreme Court, 179 judges of circuit courts of appeal, and 649 district judgeships.[57]

The scattered charges and the mixed Senate verdicts in the 13 cases when impeachment was used to remove federal judges do not permit many clear conclusions about what behavior will bring about the sanction of removal. All 13 judges were charged with the rather imprecise offense of high crimes and misdemeanors; none has been impeached for treason or bribery, even though bribery was the root charge in several instances. The Claiborne and Nixon cases make quite clear what should have been obvious previously: conviction on criminal charges is sufficient grounds for removal. Otherwise, only general kinds of behavior that might constitute impeachable offenses can be defined. Because of the unique features of each case and the historical context in which each occurred, absolute precedents cannot be derived. "High crimes and misdemeanors" was a phrase known in English law at the time the U.S. Constitution was written and referred to "misprisons," including maladministration and embezzlement.[58] Greater specificity cannot be obtained from the American experience. Black has argued that impeachable offenses are those that "are rather obviously wrong, whether or not 'criminal,' " and sufficiently serious to make "dangerous the continuance in power of their perpetrator."[59] Fenton suggests another only slightly more concrete version of transgressions that are impeachable. Based on all of the impeachments conducted in the United States, he claims that official misconduct or violation of criminal or civil law qualifies.[60] That conclusion, albeit correct, still leaves considerable elasticity in the scope of impeachable conduct. Another formula, offered by Gerhardt, focuses on the public trust. If the officeholder violates the public trust, he loses the confidence of the public and must forfeit the office.[61] That formulation, like all others based on the history of impeachment in the United States, leaves completely obscure the question of whether one can be impeached only for official conduct or whether private behavior can equally trigger the process for removal.

Canons of Judicial Ethics

The American Bar Association first formulated its Canons of Judicial Ethics in 1924 in an attempt to bolster public confidence in the courts, which it felt had been damaged by some questionable judicial activities. Besides the political scandal that was widespread in the 1920s, the so-called Black Sox scandal directly impinged on the federal judiciary.

The Black Sox, the nickname of eight players for the Chicago White Sox, were indicted in 1920, along with five professional gamblers, for allegedly conspiring to fix games and extend the influence of corrupt professional gambling into baseball. The reaction of the baseball owners was to create the office of baseball commissioner. Sitting U.S. District Judge Kenesaw Mountain Landis was tapped for the post, which he accepted without resigning from his judicial office. The American Bar Association (ABA) formally censured the judge for engaging in private employment, behavior that was "derogatory to the dignity of the Bench."[62] Amid calls for Landis's impeachment, he resigned his judgeship and served as baseball commissioner until 1944. These events have been interpreted as the catalyst for the ABA's 1924 Canons of Judicial Ethics, a codification that was never formally adopted by the federal judiciary.[63]

The 1960s again witnessed considerable publicity about federal judges and their conduct. Supreme Court Justices William O. Douglas and Abe Fortas were investigated by congressional committees and in the press; nothing came of the Douglas inquiries, but Fortas, as noted previously, resigned from the bench. The failed Supreme Court nomination of federal judge Clement Haynesworth in 1970 also raised the specter of conflict of interest on the federal courts. The ABA reacted in 1972 by writing a second version of its Canons of Judicial Ethics, which was far more precise than its 1924 forerunner. A key element in canon 4 was carried over, however, and made more restrictive: the 1924 code's requirement that a judge's official conduct be "free from impropriety and the appearance of impropriety" and that his "everyday life should be beyond reproach."[64] The 1972 version more broadly required that "a judge should avoid impropriety and the appearance of impropriety in all his activities."[65] The Watergate scandal, in which the principal actors were almost all in the legal field, prompted a surge of interest in the ethics of public officials. The 1972 ABA Code was later adopted totally by 45 states, the District of Columbia, and the governing body of the federal judiciary, and partially by the remaining five states.[66] A new set of ethics adopted by the ABA in 1990 is written in gender-neutral language that sets mandatory standards. The newest version is more precise and more restrictive than its predecessors.[67]

The intent behind the codification of ethical standards is to make clear what is and is not acceptable behavior. Undoubtedly, judges who accepted bribes or illegal gratuities, who committed perjury or evaded taxes, and who acted in an openly biased fashion on the bench were well aware that their conduct was unethical. The value of the codes is in clarifying fuzzy areas that had previously been left to individual discretion.[68] If the enforcement of the canons is left to the individual judge's sense of self-discipline, however, without the possibility of external sanction, there is no accountability.

Auxiliary Federal Measures

Justice William Rehnquist commented more than two decades ago that "if experience demands a presumption that a judge will seize every opportunity presented to him in the course of his official conduct to line his pockets, no canon of ethics or statute regarding disqualification can save our judicial system."[69] He is, of course, correct. There has been a recognition nonetheless that when a judge indeed acts venally, some method besides that of impeachment is necessary to rid the bench of the corrupt judge. In 1791 a constitutional amendment was proposed in Congress to create an alternative means of removing judges; William Randolph introduced a similar amendment after his experience with the Chase impeachment. Between 1807 and 1812, another nine were proposed that would change or limit judicial tenure, and in 1832 the House failed to pass an amendment that would have set term limits on federal judges. A bill to set a mandatory retirement age failed in Congress in 1870.[70]

In 1980 the Judicial Councils Reform and Judicial Conduct and Disability Act (hereafter referred to as Judicial Conduct Act) passed Congress and was signed into law by President Jimmy Carter. That law was designed to allow judges to monitor the conduct and competence of disabled and misbehaving peers, without resort to the cumbersome machinery of impeachment. The law was built upon a series of earlier statutes passed throughout the twentieth century that incrementally established the processes and the authority of judicial bodies to monitor judicial ranks. The gradual approach was essential, as every effort to curtail the complete discretion of any judge had been labeled an incursion into judicial independence.

The Judicial Conference was created in 1922, and the Administrative Office Act followed in 1939. Both were but small steps toward creation of bodies for the self-governance of the federal judiciary, with powers that expanded only slightly after each revision. The 1939 law, for example, created circuit councils with the authority to define and control judicial assignments. The scope of the councils was further enlarged by the 1948 revision of the Judicial Code, that allowed councils to issue direct orders instead of directives to judges; to certify physical and mental disability of judges; and to relieve judges of their caseloads, even by reassigning judges to nonexistent jurisdictions. The constitutionality of the law and of council actions under it were upheld by the Supreme Court.[71]

In 1965 a Senate subcommittee led by Joseph Tydings began a study of possible judicial reforms, and in 1975 Senator Sam Nunn assumed the mantle of judicial reformer with his Judicial Tenure Act, that eventually became the 1980 Judicial Conduct Act. The law permits anyone to file a complaint against a judge for conduct "prejudicial to the effective and expeditious administration of the business of the courts," including allegations of physical or mental disability. The complaint is filed with the chief judge of the circuit court unless he is the object of the complaint. The chief judge reviews the complaint, and a copy is sent to the judge against whom it is lodged. The chief judge may dismiss the complaint if it is frivolous, does not conform to statutory requirements, or is related to the merits of a specific case decided by the judge. The chief judge can also end the complaint if corrective actions have already been taken. If the allegation cannot be handled by these informal mechanisms, the chief judge is required to refer the complaint to an investigating committee, whom he appoints from among district and circuit judges in the circuit. The committee conducts an investigation, reports to the judicial council of the circuit, and recommends a resolution: dismiss the complaint, certify disability, urge the judge to retire voluntarily, freeze the judge's caseload, reprimand or censure the judge either publicly or privately, or, if removal might be warranted, refer the case to the Judicial Conference of the United States. That body, composed of judges elected from all of the circuits and presided over by the chief justice, may certify to the House of Representatives that impeachment may be justified.[72]

The Judicial Conduct Act took effect in 1981, and in the 10 years following its implementation 1,910 complaints were filed. The overwhelming majority of those complaints (1,379, or 72 percent) were dismissed by chief judges as not conforming to the statutory requirements, as related to the merits of the case, or as frivolous. Seventeen others were withdrawn. A total of 415 were referred to investigating committees, where all but eight were dismissed. Of the eight where an investigation indicated that some formal action was required, three resulted in recommendations for voluntary retirement; two, in private censures; one, in a public censure; one, in referral to the Judicial Conference; and one in an unspecified action. A total of 54 were handled by the chief judge in a category reported as "corrective action taken." The remaining cases were still pending in 1991.[73]

Because all allegations and investigations are confidential unless they are preludes to a public reprimand or to a referral to the House of Representatives, only aggregate information is available about complaints and their resolution. The 54 in which some corrective action had been taken may perhaps be the area where the Judicial Conduct Act has the greatest impact. A survey of the confidential files by Collins Fitzpatrick revealed that at least nine judges retired once a complaint was filed against them and that judges with physical or mental health problems assumed senior status with reduced caseloads. In cases of drinking problems or other psychological difficulties, the offending judges sought professional help. Fitzpatrick concludes that the investigations allowed by the Judicial Conduct Act likely encourage voluntary compliance, but also that many similar judicial difficulties are resolved without the stimulus of a complaint.[74]

Some light is shed on the workings of the Judicial Conduct Act by the nature of the complaints that are filed. Most are not for physical or mental infirmity: only 58 alleging mental incompetency and 23 concerning physical disability were received in the 10 years following the act. The largest number (1,510) related to unethical behavior (demeanor, abuse of judicial power, prejudice or bias, conflict of interest, and corruption). A total of 509 involved basic competency: undue decisional delay and neglect or incompetence. The remaining grievances fit into none of the categories specified in the statute.

The few cases that reached the press despite the guarantees of confidentiality offer some insights into the nature of the investigating process. Judge Miles Lord of Minnesota was investigated in 1984 because of his comments to the corporate officers of A.H. Robins Company after the company had reached a settlement agreement regarding the company's sale of the unsafe Dalkon Shield intrauterine device. Judge Lord, who was presiding over the case, publicly reprimanded the corporate officers for irresponsible behavior; the officers replied with a complaint filed with the chief judge of the Eighth Judicial Circuit. After a seven-month investigation that cost Judge Lord $70,000 in legal fees, the investigating committee recommended that the complaint be dismissed. Judge Lord resigned from the bench less than a year later.[75] In addition, the full record of the Alcee Hastings investigation is public; it is the only report of a recommendation to the judicial conference by an investigating committee. Harry Claiborne's case was not investigated by his circuit council even though possible impeachment was warranted. In his case, the certification by the Judicial Conference to the House of Representatives was accomplished by a conference call among all of the judges elected to that body. They concurred that Claiborne's conviction negated any requirement for a separate investigation.[76]

The viability of impeachment, supplemented by the Judicial Conduct Act, for deterring and punishing judicial misbehavior cannot be precisely weighed. Some judges on the federal bench have undoubtedly deserved removal because of improper conduct or mental or physical incapacity. That so few have been removed directly through impeachment and even fewer through public actions of the judicial councils might be regarded as an indictment of the system. Three times the number removed resigned when investigations were initiated, and many others may have left quietly because of investigations that were pending or because of pressure from friends and colleagues. That the U.S. bench tends to maintain substantial legitimacy in the eyes of lawyers practicing before it suggests that at least the very worst and most dangerous judges responded to confidential nudges and left the bench.

State Systems

The federal principle in the United States grants to each state total autonomy in its choices of court organization and methods for recruiting, disciplining, and removing judges. The variety of schemes devised to govern the approximately 30,000 state court judges is vast. This heterogeneity was not always the case, however. Eleven of the original 13 states drafted constitutions in 1776, while Rhode Island continued its 1663 British charter; Massachusetts completed its state constitution in 1780. Colonial experiences with Crown judges had instilled a fear of executive control of the judiciary in those writing the new state constitutions, and not one permitted the governor to appoint judges unilaterally. Seven states placed the appointing authority in the legislature. In the remaining states, gubernatorial appointment required concurrence of the legislature or of a legislative council. Most allowed removal by a simple majority vote in those assemblies.[77] Judges were generally granted tenure for good behavior; New Jersey and Pennsylvania specified terms but permitted renewals. Every new state that was added to the Union until 1845 used either legislative appointment or gubernatorial appointment, conditioned by legislative or legislative council confirmation.[78]

The election of Andrew Jackson as president ushered in a new era of democratic accountability for all public officials, including judges. Lower court judges in Georgia had been elected since 1812, and Mississippi changed its constitution in 1832 to permit election of all judges.[79] The political patronage that usually characterized judicial appointments was one explanation for the change; another was the difficulty of removing undesirable judges. Three consecutive Mississippi legislatures had been unsuccessful in their attempts to impeach Supreme Court Justice Joshua Child, who had been charged with dueling, drunkenness, various acts of official misconduct, and, perhaps most important, declaring an act of the Mississippi legislature unconstitutional in 1824. Frustration with impeachment spurred the adoption of partisan elections.[80] Kentucky was similarly unhappy with the impeachment mechanism for ridding the bench of judges who were too independent. Frustrated at failing to muster the two-thirds majority needed to impeach judges of the court of appeal for declaring a law unconstitutional, the Kentucky legislature in 1823 abolished the court entirely.[81]

New York followed the example of Mississippi in 1846 and the trend toward electing judges was begun. Eighteen additional states made the change before 1861, and every new state entering the union until 1912 opted for electing judicial personnel. Around the turn of the twentieth century, however, perceptions that the courts were overly political led to the introduction of nonpartisan elections. The logic was simple and straightforward: parties equal politics; remove political parties and thereby insulate the courts from politics. Elections remain, despite their many critics, the primary method for selecting judges in the American states. In 1993, 20 states used partisan, and 19 states nonpartisan, elections to select judges for at least one level of court. If the minor courts are excluded, partisan elections can be found in only 12 states.

Myriad criticisms are leveled at elective procedures for selecting judges. The obvious one is the potential damage to judicial independence. The more relevant argument against elective procedures to remove unfit judges, however, is that it is ineffective. The single outstanding feature of elections is that incumbent judges are not turned out of office.[82] Indeed, most sitting judges do not even draw opposition, and for those who do, electoral success is the most likely outcome. When an incumbent is defeated, it is because potential challengers knew that the judge was vulnerable.[83] Or, put more bluntly, an incumbent judge draws opposition because of publicized incompetency or other public shortcomings.[84] As judgeships are typically low-visibility positions, voters have little information to guide their decisions.[85] The opposing argument is that those voters who do not "roll off" before reaching the judgeships on the ballot are self-selected and well-informed, the kind who should decide the fate of judicial officers.[86] Many voters rely, however, on cues that can be discerned within the four corners of the ballot, and if incumbency is indicated, its importance is even greater in garnering votes.[87]

Another condemnation of elections for selecting or removing judges focuses on campaign finances. Since lawyers or others with litigation before the courts are the group most likely to donate to judicial elections, there is a risk of the appearance of buying favor on the bench.[88] An analysis of contributions to the 122 judicial races in California in 1980 revealed, however, that the average contribution was only $176 and 90 percent of all contributions were $250 or less.[89] Similarly, a study of judicial campaign finance among 86 candidates in Cook County, Illinois, in 1984 found that winning candidates spent approximately $24,000 on their races, and much of that came from the candidates' own pockets.[90] Even on a statewide scale, North Carolina Supreme Court contests were found to be relatively inexpensive propositions, particularly if viewed on a cost-per-vote basis.[91] Most analysts of judicial campaign financing approach the issue from the ethical perspective, the appearance of impropriety that results from reliance on lawyers' contributions to run in a contested election.[92] Even if elections can be mounted with very little money, should the candidates' qualifications for judgeships and fitness for office be determined by financial ability to get the message to the voters?

A final question remains regarding the efficacy of elective systems for removing the unfit judge: do partisan or nonpartisan elections work better? Partisan elections have traditionally been characterized as tainted by the influence of parties. Given the limited information available to voters and the electorate's reliance on cues, however, the other side argues that political party labels provide meaningful cues. The party affiliation of a judicial candidate at least conveys to most voters something about that person's broad orientation,[93] and no more information than that is usually available in various other elective contests.[94] In that sense, partisan elections may actually serve well to ensure judicial accountability, even if not judicial ethics.

Future use of elections to fill judicial posts may, however, be altered somewhat by judicial interpretation of the 1965 Voting Rights Act, as amended in 1982. The law and subsequent amendment were designed to eliminate discriminatory results in election procedures, in particular those that result from gerrymandering of electoral districts along racial or ethnic lines. The U.S. Supreme Court in 1991 concluded that judicial elections are also covered by the act.[95] A host of lawsuits in several states were filed thereafter, and many have been settled by consent decrees. The long-term impact of resolutions to guarantee that racial and ethnic minorities do not have their votes diluted at the ballot box may alter how judges are elected.

The merit selection/merit retention system was conceived in its basic outline form by Professor Albert Kales of Northwestern University[96] and was endorsed by the American Bar Association in 1937. Its basic component is a nominating commission to screen potential judges and to submit a list to an elected official who then appoints a judge to serve for some fixed time; at the conclusion of that probationary period, the judge runs in a noncompetitive election to determine continuance for an additional term. Professor Kales's plan used a nominating commission of presiding judges, but in most states where the plan has been adopted, representatives of the legal community and lay people are included. The commission was designed to ensure the qualifications of the candidates, and the retention elections are to allow for public accountability. The latter aspect is the one of concern here.

Merit selection/retention has gained widespread support among legal professionals but has not been equally popular with the public. California was the first state to adopt the system, in 1934, and was followed by Missouri in 1940. Twenty-two states currently use some variation of this basic plan for initial selection to some level of courts; 32 use merit selection to fill midterm vacancies. The differences among the states are substantial. In some instances, merit selection is followed by competitive elections or by other types of electoral participation depending on length of service on the bench. There are two peculiar features of retention elections that separate them from the typical election. First, no one may run against the candidate judge; second, in some states more than a simple majority is required for continuance in office. In the first 45 years that the plan was in operation, only 33 judges were removed through retention elections, and most of those (25) were defeated for significant reasons, ranging from criminal activity, scandals, and incompetence to controversial decisions and local politics.[97] The reluctance of voters to turn out judges in retention elections increases the natural advantage of incumbents, with the result that more than 97 percent of sitting judges win these elections each year.[98] One study of the 1,864 retention contests in 10 states from 1964 through 1984 found that only 22 sitting judges were defeated.[99] The system rather effectively insulates judges from the electorate, and only the rare judicial animal has less than life tenure in office. Defenders of merit retention argue that this is how the plan was intended to operate. Because of the merit selection procedures, only well-qualified judges should be named; lengthy tenure is to be expected unless an egregious offense is committed. That small number of judges turned out by the voters is an indication that the system works well. And that some judges are removed demonstrates that public accountability is present but untainted by partisanship, money, or campaigns.[100] On the other hand, voters apparently do not clearly differentiate among judges, and their decisions on the judiciary as a whole tend to reflect swings in political trust more than an evaluation of an individual judge's fitness for office.[101]

Judicial Conduct Organizations

Each of the systems used to appoint and remove judges in the American states—elections, appointment, and merit systems—are now supplemented by judicial conduct organizations. This fact represents at least a tacit recognition that the other mechanisms created to monitor judicial conduct are insufficient. The major limitations of the other methods lie in the lack of time or resources to investigate complaints. This deficiency led to the establishment in 1947 of the New York Court of the Judiciary, which was subsequently abandoned. In 1960 California instituted its Judicial Qualifications Commission as an adjunct to the judicial branch, and every other state and the District of Columbia have by now followed that lead. These commissions, generically called judicial conduct organizations, typically screen and investigate complaints and make recommendations for action to the state supreme court. In 43 states and the District of Columbia a single commission, a mix of lawyers, judges, and lay people, handles all three functions, while in seven states the screening or investigating functions are separated from hearings and recommendations.[102] Generally, commissions are authorized to issue subpoenas, to compel sworn testimony and production of physical evidence, and to seek court orders to force compliance. In virtually every state, the commissions may merely recommend; usually the state supreme court, or in a few rare cases the state legislature, holds the ultimate power of sanction.[103]

Each state establishes different standards for its judges and prescribes appropriate penalties. The 1972 ABA Code of Judicial Conduct has been adopted by 45 states, but Illinois, Maryland, Montana, Rhode Island, and Wisconsin have codes of ethics that are significantly different.[104] Generally speaking, the codes require impartiality, knowledge of the law, courteous and dignified behavior, and diligence.[105] Variations on those themes in practice, however, make generalizations somewhat difficult. Some states are noted for being aggressive. In New York, for example, the judicial conduct organization initiated proceedings that resulted in the removal of 75 judges in a mere 12 years. California is noted, on the other hand, for its laxness in punishing judicial misconduct.[106] The general assumption is, however, that most judicial conduct organizations are reluctant to expose judges publicly.[107] The record of the Illinois commission in 1988–89 is quite typical. A substantial number of complaints were received (155), and 148 were dismissed. One judge resigned after an investigation began and two received public discipline; the remaining cases were handled through informal actions.[108] Similarly, 36 state commissions in 1983 reported a total of almost 4,500 complaints received, but only 50 resulted in resignations or retirements, and 107 were handled with a censure or reprimand.[109] Commissioners responded that the number of complaints that are frivolous or that simply dispute a judge's decision in a case are far more common than are serious charges. The confidentiality of commission investigations is intended to shield the reputations of judges who are accused unjustly. Some states do not even have set criteria for imposing sanctions, and in reality most might as well not have any because of the inevitably unique facts that emerge in every case.[110] Removals, as a rule, occur only after multiple instances of misconduct on the bench or "repeated and flagrant" misbehavior off the bench.[111] Even though the commissions are often accused of lacking the courage to remove unfit judges, 183 were removed through judicial conduct organization initiatives from 1980 through 1991.[112]

Assessments

The diversity of practices for disciplining and removing judges in the United States makes any kind of overall evaluation or summation impractical. Impeachment at either the state or the national level intrudes upon the legislative agenda so dramatically that it fell into disuse, and other judicial branch mechanisms were created to act in lieu of the legislature. This shift of functions has apparently worked rather effectively, at least in saving legislative time in the states, but it has not relieved Congress of the cumbersome task at the national level. Elections have not necessarily removed unfit judges from the state benches, as demonstrated repeatedly, and life tenure until mandatory retirement seems almost the norm where elections—partisan, nonpartisan or retention—are used.

A willingness to experiment with new and alternative approaches to ensuring judicial accountability sets the United States apart from other nations considered. As more and more disputes are litigated and the ranks of lawyers continue to swell, additional judgeships will be necessary. The difficulties in monitoring the conduct of some 31,000 judges at this time will be further aggravated as that number grows. Very likely, however, some inventive soul in one of the states will advance another theory or devise another scheme to confront the question of judicial accountability. Some state legislature will permit it to be tested if it appears to be an improvement on the existing system, and if it is viable, other states will adopt, modify, and introduce additional innovations. The tension between assumptions underlying judicial independence versus judicial accountability remains relatively unchanged in the United States since the nineteenth century, but the ways of balancing and achieving the two are in a seemingly persistent state of transformation and renewal.

Chapter 6

Judging the Judges

Four nations, closely related in many respects, illustrate historically at least eight examples of approaches to the dilemma of judicial accountability. Though the French system of venality practiced under the Ancien Régime and the Italian schemes under the monarchy and under fascism are not likely to be resurrected for present or future use in democratic structures, they are nonetheless instructive about the nature of judicial accountability in democratic, predemocratic, and authoritarian regimes. The historical overviews of France, Italy, Britain, and the United States highlight the considerable variations that exist even among democratic nations sharing the same legal and political roots.

What is most remarkably apparent from our country-by-country examination is that very few judges are removed from the bench for any reason. The various judicial conduct organizations in the American states, often operating in tandem with formal systems for electing judges, have been the most active in stripping errant judges of their positions. Even so, the almost 200 state judges who over the last 10 years received the most severe punishment—formal removal—represent only a tiny fraction of the approximately 30,000 judges serving on state benches. That 10-year figure of 200, moreover, exceeds the total number of magistrates (judges and prosecutors) in France, Italy, and U.S. federal courts, plus English judges, taken from their offices this century.

An appealing explanation is that judges in democracies comport themselves with such honor and dignity and decide all cases so impartially that no discipline is necessary. The overwhelming majority undoubtedly do so. Nevertheless, in a two-week period in late 1993, newspapers reported that the chief justice of the Rhode Island Supreme Court was under investigation for ethical improprieties,[1] that the chief judge of New York State was awaiting criminal sentencing on charges that he had threatened to kidnap the daughter of a former romantic liaison,[2] and that the Italian CSM was suspending the former president of the Milan tribunal for allegations of corruption[3] and was trying to clear a backlog of investigations involving 119 magistrates.[4]

Anecdotal and idiographic descriptions of the cases of individual judges allow events to be considered in context, but examples such as the ones just cited do not move us any closer to explaining, much less resolving, the apparent paradox that judges represent in democratic societies. The preceding four chapters describe how judges have been held accountable historically, and, rich with detail, they are instructive about how individual nations have in different eras addressed the question. The discrepancies and similarities among the nations considered can best be examined from the perspective of the model proposed in the introductory chapter of this book. Judicial status, legal culture, political environment, and judicial authority were proposed as independent variables that jointly influence mechanisms for monitoring judicial conduct and setting expectations of acceptable judicial behavior. These last two factors would, in turn, influence judicial accountability. Only when the original model is examined in light of information from each of the nations considered can the final and perhaps most important questions be addressed: can judicial accountability can be reconciled with democratic expectations and, if so, how?

Judicial Status

Judicial elites may parallel or diverge from the development of other political elites in democratic societies; whereas the transformation of other political elites has been explored, there is little information on judicial officeholders cross-nationally.[5] That absence is lamentable because the recruitment of judges is the key point where the judiciary and a nation's culture meet, and it serves as the "means to reinforce old values and inculcate new ones through the socialization of decision-makers."[6] The mechanism by which judges are named and the types of people who are attracted to judicial positions are indicative of the status of judges in a nation.

Under the Ancien Régime in France, judges bought their offices, though the positions were prized more for social purposes than as investments.

There was even then a system in place whereby candidates who wanted to purchase an office called on members of the court to secure their favorable votes. Though that custom eventually paled into insignificance, it is emblematic of the relatively high status that judges held and wanted to preserve during the predemocratic period.[7]

Recruitment of the judiciary in England in parallel times mirrored the generally high level of prestige that attached to French judicial offices, but recruitment followed a different format. A kind of professional judiciary can be traced to the reign of Henry III in the mid-thirteenth century, and the status of royal judges was further enhanced by the rise of professionalism among lawyers that coincided with the establishment of the Inns of Court at the end of that century. Judges were, nonetheless, the king's judges—appointed and removed at his pleasure.

Judges in Italy under the monarchy and the Fascist regime were also the king's men, for justice was administered in his name. There was relatively little room for judicial maneuvering under the monarchy and even less under Fascism, when the Grand Fascist Council became a player in the discipline and removal of judges. The positions were part of the civil service, however, and carried a fair amount of status and security in this predemocratic era of Italian history.

With the shift from pre- or protodemocratic epochs, recruitment patterns shifted, but the status of judges did not seem to diminish. The short-lived revolutionary period in France saw the quick rise and rapid demise of an elective process for naming judges, who were not even required to be trained in the law. At a roughly concurrent time in the United States, judges at both the state and national levels were appointed; most of the original 13 states, however, distrusted unbridled judicial discretion and imposed term limitations. The prestige of the federal judiciary was not, at least initially, alluring enough to attract or retain the best of the legal community, but with time that pattern altered. Federal judgeships are generally regarded as the pinnacle of the legal profession, and though state judicial positions are given mixed assessments, they are generally accorded a fairly high status.

Napoleon created the civil service model for judicial recruitment in France, and it has persisted with some modification into the Fifth Republic. The system is characterized by executive appointment and secure tenure, despite a number of purges that accompanied volatile regime changes in the nineteenth century.[8] The establishment at the beginning of the Fifth Republic of an institute for training magistrates, now the École

Nationale de la Magistrature (ENM), has lent the magistrature a greater aura of professionalism and has secured a common socialization for judges. Like other parts of the French bureaucracy that form the *grands corps,* the magistrature is granted a relatively high status.[9]

The postwar Republic of Italy followed the French lead in creating a magistrature along a civil service model, but the Italian version provides for even greater insulation from executive interference than its French counterpart. There is no special training for recruits to the Italian judiciary, and the hierarchical civil service model carries less prestige than the French version, in part because of the absence of merit considerations in promotions and the ability of magistrates to serve in other government positions. Public appraisals of the magistrature have been inconsistent, with higher prestige attaching to the profession when other institutions of government are seen as besieged, but waning quickly when political equilibrium seems to exist.

English judges, at least those on the higher courts, probably command the highest levels of respect among those we have considered. Judges are appointed only after having achieved substantial success as barristers, and they are remunerated handsomely, at least in comparison with French, Italian, and American judges, for leaving the practice of law to assume a place on the bench.[10] They are similarly drawn from the higher echelons of society, as measured by their fathers' occupations and their own educational backgrounds.[11] Though appointments are made by politicians, even the most aggressive critics of the English bench concede that selection is nonpartisan.

Legal Culture

The basic assumptions that underlie the civil law versus the common law traditions would suggest that expectations of judicial performance would be different under each type of legal culture. The notion of civil law has at its base a belief that the legislature has written the law, formalized in codes, and that the judge serves only as the mouth of the law. Common law, on the other hand, presumes interpretation by judges in the application of law to specific cases. It overtly and explicitly recognizes the power of judicial interpretation to give direction and meaning to laws. Those differences in practice are more illusory than real, as civil law judges are frequently called upon to read between the lines of codes and to extrapolate from the general principles provided and as common law judges frequently find little or no room left for discretion in the language of the statutes.

The common law as practiced in England stands at some distance from its American version, moreover, largely because of parliamentary sovereignty in England and judicial review in the United States. English judges are prohibited, except as required by adherence to the European Community, from directly confronting, much less overruling, an act of Parliament. The American practice of decentralized judicial review, on the other hand, empowers even the lowest judge to declare legislative acts invalid. That distinction may have greater relevance for judicial accountability than the civil versus common law distinction.

Even so, the assumptions undergirding civil and common law, however much at variance with reality they may be, form and mold expectations about the limits of judicial power. Judges who are conceived by other branches of government and by the public as servants of the law, *la bouche . . . de la loi, des êtres inanimés* (the mouth of the law, dead beings), are not treated as serious threats to executive or legislative prerogatives. The absence of accountability assumes less relevance if the judges possess no political will. The legal culture that surrounds common law judges would appear, on the other hand, to demand some form of democratic accountability. These judges are largely chosen through political processes, in clear recognition of their political role.[12]

Political Environment

The general political environment in which judges operate is a determining factor in limiting their sphere of operation and defining the relationship of the judiciary to the remainder of the political system. This is true whether judges are viewed as political actors or not. Under the French monarchy during the Ancien Régime and under the English one until 1761, judges were part of the political system. In the English experience, *rex* was *lex*, with the possible exception of the Tudor period. There was virtually no opposition to the monarchy from among the judicial ranks, all of whom in England and France benefited from the system of rank and class. One explanation for the rise of independent judiciaries in France and England during this time, while contemporary institutions struggled against monarchal absolutism, is that the rule of law was an essential element of "the self-interested and wealth-maximizing behavior of rulers and their subjects."[13] This led to a number of constitutional contracts, among them an independent judiciary. Rulers needed to contract with subjects for taxes and other revenue, but they could only persuade subjects to enter into these arrangements if there was a judge whom the subjects could trust would not always rule in the king's favor. Monarchs were, following this logic, willing to cede some power to independent judges and to the rule of law.[14] This explanation is undoubtedly only partially complete, but the fact remains that judges in both France and England acted independently at times during the predemocratic stage. To some extent, the same might be said of judges in predemocratic Italy. The monarchy held sway over the judges before and during the Fascist period, and there was little or no opposition to the regime among the magistrates, but there was still a semblance of judicial independence or at least impartiality. The best evidence of this was the decision of the Fascist regime to try political cases in special tribunals separate from the regular courts.

In England there was a gradual evolution toward ending Crown or government control of the judiciary that culminated in 1761 with the guarantee of life tenure for judges. The French ended the monarchy by revolution and experienced frequent changes of regime until the creation of the Fifth Republic in 1958. Napoleon's reforms of the judiciary, which established the beginnings of the civil service regiment, lent a stability to the magistrature that lasted through six changes in form of government in the nineteenth century, but even so some purges of judges occurred. The judiciary remained, despite guarantees of irremovability, subject to the executive for appointment and through the minister of justice for continuance in office.

The United States, like England, experienced little internal turmoil outside the years of the Civil War. Though the two major parties rotated in and out of power, there were no dramatic shifts in the political environment. The pragmatic and narrow range of moderate political ideologies that so typify American politics left the judiciary largely untouched. Clashes between the Jeffersonians and the Federalists on the nation's benches were manifested in two impeachment trials. There have also been other instances when the sitting administration has publicly disagreed with the Supreme Court, most notably during the Jacksonian era, during the New Deal, and more recently under Court-fashioned policies on regulating abortion and on school busing to achieve racial integration. These disagreements rarely resulted in direct attacks on the judiciary and were usually narrowly focused on the Supreme Court. The U.S. political environment has not been hostile to the judiciary, in other words, nor have individual administrations used explicit threats or direct coercion to influence the nation's judges.

Judicial Authority

The authority that courts may exercise can perhaps best be grasped by using the two separate dimensions defined by Carlo Guarnieri. The first is the degree of autonomy that judges have in their fields of action, and the second is the scope allowed for exercise of discretion or creativity. Using those two criteria, you may recall, judges can be classified as guardians when autonomy is high but the discretion allowed is limited. Those judges with both a low level of independence and minimal room for creativity were labeled as executors, who are faithful to the command of the legislature and are passive rather than active. The opposite extreme is the political judge, who has been granted both high autonomy and high discretion. The final category is the delegate judge, whose autonomy is low but whose potential for creativity is high. These distinctions are particularly useful for grouping the judges in our study.

Judges under the French Ancien Régime had total autonomy from the monarch, as they could not be removed. At the same time, however, they could be punished (and rather severely) for their actions by their fellow judges. The institution of the judiciary was quite independent, in other words, despite the stipulation that no individual judge could act with impunity. That autonomy was not fully matched by the level of discretion permitted, since opposition to the monarch was not considered possible. When the judicial parliaments in fact issued remonstrances to the king, they were not always well received. French judges during this predemocratic period most closely fit the guardian category. Guarnieri linked that label to contemporary notions of judges who use the judicial power to preserve fundamental human rights; such a conception would be quite inappropriate during the Ancien Régime. The guardian judges were instead inclined to preserve the status quo, as a kind of predemocratic constitution.

Early English judges were described as lions under the throne. Their sphere of discretion in fashioning the common law was quite broad, except when it encroached upon the monarchy. The Tudor period was marked by less monarchal meddling with judicial affairs, and judges were believed to act apolitically. Even so, they served at the pleasure of the Crown and therefore had little autonomy and limited discretion. They would most closely fit the description of the executor judge, passively serving as the mouth of parliamentary law and only filling in between the lines. The same term would apply to Italian judges under the monarchy and under Fascism, for they were characterized by executive domination and administrative status; interpretation of the law was a legislative prerogative. Under Mussolini, so that no judge might be tempted to decide contrary to the wishes of the government, political cases were removed from the jurisdiction of the ordinary courts.

The advent of democratic regimes altered the place of judges in France, England, and Italy. English judges were granted total autonomy during the reign of George III in 1761, when their tenure changed to that of good behavior, independent of the life of the appointing monarch. Security of salary completed the guarantee of independence. The level of discretion allowed to English judges is, however, mixed. Their role in the formation of the common law, noted previously, provides them with no small measure of authority. At the same time, the doctrine of parliamentary sovereignty severely restricts the sphere of their actions. Though that doctrine remains firmly intact, judges in England have gained a wedge in the door of political power through a particular administrative remedy that can be invoked when public authority is unfairly or abusively used. The procedure, called "judicial review," bears no resemblance to the power that the term usually connotes to an American reader. Furthermore, compliance with English obligations under the European Union has necessitated that judges measure parliamentary enactments against the requirements of European law. Though judicial review and compliance with the European Union might eventually alter the scope of authority for English judges, their currently limited discretion and complete independence would argue for classifying them as guardians, acting to ensure fundamental principles.

Since the Napoleonic reforms that began in 1799, judges in France have clearly been guardians. Their total autonomy is ensured by their irremovability; their authority, considerably curtailed by the formal renunciation of a judicial power. There is in France only a judicial function, not a power. Though judges are no longer generally described as the mere mouth of the law, the range of their power is definitely circumscribed.

The Italian republic borrowed heavily from the French in designing its postwar judiciary, but Italian magistrates are far more autonomous and have greater discretion than their French counterparts. These magistrates also work in a civil service model and are likewise denied the power of judicial review; there is a similar separation from the administrative court system. Italian magistrates have, nonetheless, earned a reputation for wielding discretion and reading parliamentary laws creatively. Their reading of their own role distinguishes them from French magistrates. That differentiation can be explained by the constitutional recognition of a judicial power in Italy. The Italian courts are not daily and consistently involved in the political life of the country, but in certain specific periods they have been quite active through criminal prosecutions and civil trials. This role can be seen in the early days of the republic, when courts vigorously pursued prosecutions against those accused of anticlerical crimes; in the 1970s against terrorist groups; in the 1980s in the investigation of the P-2 Masonic Lodge; and in the 1990s in the political corruption investigations. Italian magistrates fit better in the category of guardians, with high autonomy and low creativity. At the same time, because the Italian magistrature is highly politicized, as is quite obvious from its several visibly partisan unions, and because of its intermittent forays into political justice through criminal proceedings, it might occasionally merit the classification of political for its overt involvement in policy-making.

U.S. courts, both state and local, are readily acknowledged to be not only highly autonomous but also quite political. They clearly enter the policy-making arena regularly in interpretation and application of the law, by legislating through the common law and by exercising the power of judicial review. The independence of federal judges is likely somewhat higher than that of judges on state courts, but most American judges effectively have life tenure. The Supreme Court, as the final arbiter in matters of constitutionality, has wielded the power of judicial review sparingly; only about 140 national laws have been invalidated by that court in more than 200 years. Such restraint has not characterized its review of state legislative actions; more than 1,000 state laws have been struck down in the twentieth century alone.[15] State courts also hold the power of judicial review and, though the aggregate number of state laws invalidated by their own tribunals is not available, this procedure has been frequently employed.

The judges of France, England, Italy, and the United States, particularly if viewed from a historical perspective, are quite different from one another with respect to the authority that they possess. Notably, the executor judge, the weakest type, is not found among any of the democratic regimes and is but a historical relic from predemocratic eras. Nor are there delegate judges, having low autonomy and high creativity. Rather, judges in the Western democracies considered here all have considerable independence, and variations relate to the creativity or discretion that is allowed them.

Monitoring Mechanisms

The original model proposed that judicial status, legal culture, the political environment, and judicial authority would combine to influence both the type of monitoring mechanisms that are available to police erring judges and the nature of the ethical norms enforced for magistrates. The effects of the four independent variables will become clear in discussions of each. Mauro Cappelletti's classification scheme for methods of monitoring judicial behavior or ensuring judicial accountability offers a useful organizing device. The first category in his taxonomy is political accountability, in which judges are responsible for their conduct either to the political branches or to the constitution. The American process of impeachment and its antecedent in England from 1388 until the nineteenth century are clearly within this category, as is the current English provision for removal by address of both houses of Parliament. Both approaches place authority squarely in the legislative branch, and the process is strictly political, not legal. This placement of the policing power over judicial personnel, though, seems to ensure that it will not be used. Only seven federal judges in the United States have been removed through impeachment in more than 200 years, and only once, in 1830, has an English judge lost his office through address. Charges have been introduced in the legislative branch on both sides of the Atlantic on a number of occasions, but legislators have been disinclined to censure accused judges. English judges, for example, have escaped parliamentary reproach as long as there is an absence of corrupt motives, despite egregious judicial conduct in some instances. In the United States the conclusion is that no judge would be called to the bar of Congress, at least in the last 50 years, unless he had obviously been involved in criminal conduct. In none of the four countries we have considered has the responsibility for monitoring judicial conduct been placed exclusively in the executive, though that organ of government shares a role in other systems of monitoring.

Societal or public accountability, according to Cappelletti, enables the people to remove judges in a more direct fashion, as dramatically illustrated in fourteenth-century England, when mobs seized and executed at least two judges for failing to meet their expectations. Elections, the most democratically acceptable mechanisms of public accountability, were practiced briefly during the revolutionary era in France, and they are currently used in a majority of the American states. Recall elections, as well as retention elections that follow merit selection schemes, are now available in a number of American states. These practices are wholly consistent with democratic norms, despite the variety of complaints associated with them.

Cappelletti also includes exposure of judges to public criticism, usually through the mass media but also in specialist literature, as a form of public accountability. All of the nations we have considered, at least in their democratic incarnations, protect and guarantee press freedoms and therefore permit public scrutiny of judicial actions. But judges can ignore public disagreement with their decisions or their comportment; there is no definitive sanction that accompanies expressions of dissatisfaction in the media. The media exercises, rather, an indirect influence, acting as a catalyst for other players. Negative media publicity, for example, has been a critical factor in causing sitting judges to lose elections in the American states.[16]

Vicarious state liability allows a litigant to seek damages for injuries caused by the actions of a judge acting in an official capacity, in addition to any civil or criminal liability of the individual judge. The focus in this type of accountability is legal, not political, and it therefore differs considerably from public or political accountability; the emphasis is on violations of the law, not on "politically or socially reprovable behavior."[17] In the United States, judicial errors generally cannot be corrected through state liability, although various technical rules govern the ability of an individual to seek reparations from the state for judicial wrongdoing. The same general principle applies with reference to English judges. In France, on the other hand, only the state may be held liable; there is no personal liability for judicial officers.[18] In Italy since 1988, litigants similarly can sue the state for compensation for judicial wrongs. In Italy there is also provision for what Cappelletti refers to as "recovery liability," whereby the state may subsequently recover from the offending judge some of the damages it is assessed. The focus of each of these systems is not, however, on achieving judicial accountability, but rather on protecting judges from harassing and vexing lawsuits. Judicial independence is primary; compensation for a victim of an erroneous or malicious decision, secondary.

Cappelletti's other category of mechanisms for imposing judicial accountability is the personal legal liability of the judge. In none of the countries we have studied may judges be held civilly liable for actions taken in the course of official duties. The law as it relates to lower court judges in England was not clarified until 1979, when the shield against civil liability for lower court judges was recognized so long as the judges were acting within their jurisdictions and no malice was proved. Italian law allows for lawsuits, but the state not the individual judge assumes responsibility, though the state may recover from the offending magistrate. Personal liability for criminal actions, on the other hand, is possible in England, France, Italy, and the United States. In France under the Ancien Régime the corporation of judges tried and punished their peers for criminal acts, and the punishments were typically twofold, one for the criminal action and one for the attendant offense to the judicial office. In contemporary times, both Italian and American judges have been targets of criminal investigations and trials. Magistrates have typically resigned when investigated or at least when convicted. The glaring exceptions are the two U.S. judges who refused to resign even when convicted of criminal behavior, and a third who continued in office during a trial in which he was acquitted by a jury. All three were ultimately removed through the impeachment process, as discussed in chapter 5.

Disciplinary sanctions are a subset of Cappelletti's personal liability for judges. He notes that mechanisms for disciplining judges, aside from those just mentioned, can easily degenerate into a form of political accountability because of executive interference, or into a form of corporate control exercised by the judiciary alone.[19] Several of the historical monitoring mechanisms in England, France, Italy, and the United States cannot avoid the label of either corporate or executive control. Each appears more appropriately placed under the category of "political" or "constitutional" accountability. The rationale for this deviation from Cappelletti's model is that each of the other monitoring mechanisms has a constitutional basis that aims at a more efficient administration of the judicial system, as well as providing disciplinary rigor. The early English system for policing judicial ranks, for example, permitted Parliament to impeach, convict, remove, and punish members of the judiciary, but historically the process was marked by monarchal interference in the execution of sentences. Similarly, the corporation of judges under the Ancien Régime tried and punished their own members even when the charges included such criminal offenses as extortion, embezzlement, or even murder. The king could intercede, as he apparently did, to grant clemency, thereby injecting a political element.

Among the later democratic regimes in the United States, France, and Italy, indirect executive involvement remains an element in disciplining judges. The Napoleonic reforms in France retained the Ancien Régime model of accountability to the corporation of judges, but the executive was given a role by including the minister of justice in the process. The Fourth

Republic modified that system by creating the Superior Council of the Magistrature, which included not only judges and the minister of justice but also notables. A concrete link to the body politick was established. At the same time, magistrates of the prosecution department were no longer to be disciplined like their counterparts on the bench; they were subject to the minister of justice, who was required only to consult with an agency representing different constituencies. The Fifth Republic preserved the CSM title and its membership of mixed composition. The prosecution department continued under the supervision of the minister of justice, with an advisory function assigned to the Commission de Discipline du Parquet that included seven magistrates from the prosecution.

The 1948 Italian constitution followed the French lead and placed judicial discipline for both the bench and the prosecution under the surveillance of its CSM, also a mixed body, in which the magistrates hold a two-thirds majority. The president of the republic and the minister of justice are also members, though not part of the discipline process. Thus, a hybrid model has emerged that combines discipline of judges by their peers with a tie to the executive branch. The political character of both the French and Italian institutions is undeniable. At the same time, however, that political influence does not involve democratically accountable representatives, as do the American and English procedures for impeachment and address.

American responses to judicial discipline can be described as a creative blend of political accountability through impeachment, public responsibility through the various electoral devices, and a system of mixed or judicial supervision. Impeachment has been supplemented at the national level with peer review under the Judicial Conduct and Disability Act of 1980, whereby judges investigate and make recommendations regarding their fellows. Removal is retained as the prerogative of Congress alone, but the corporation of judges can impose lesser sanctions. Public accountability in the states has been augmented by judicial conduct organizations that are akin to the Superior Councils of the Magistrature in France and Italy. These are mixed bodies, representing usually the bench, the bar, and the public; the state governor typically appoints some members to such organizations. The result is that in France, Italy, and the United States, the bodies that have primary responsibility for receiving complaints about judicial actions borrow from the Ancien Régime practice of judges supervising other judges and from the pre-1761 English practice of political involvement of the executive. Of the contemporary models we have considered, only the English one makes judges subject solely to political accountability, through address of both houses of Parliament, or, in the case of lower court judges, to direct executive accountability, since they are removable by the lord chancellor.

Ethical Norms

Some means of policing judicial conduct in three of our countries demonstrate a degree of convergence, but some codes of conduct that govern judges are seemingly distinct in each of the four. What appears on the surface to be different, however, may represent only a thin veneer of linguistic variation. The offenses for which judges can be punished tend to fall into three broad categories. The first is political corruption, which in the case of the judiciary implies a political bias in decision-making or in public behavior. It "violates and undermines the norms of the system of public order which is deemed indispensable for the maintenance of political democracy."[20] The particular gravity of political corruption within the judicial ranks motivated Dupin in the early nineteenth century to introduce the concept of political reserve, which prohibited judges from articulating a political disposition in any public forum. The strictures have been far more loosely applied in Italy, England, and the United States, where political ties of judges are typically acknowledged. Even so, political bias that interferes with a judge's impartial administration of the law is typically regarded as an abuse of power.

A second category of offenses, personal corruption, obviously encompasses all criminal offenses. Extortion, bribery, and solicitation of illegal gratuities, for example, directly undermine the impartiality of judges. But because judges are particularly vulnerable to accusations that their impartiality has been compromised, they are often restricted as to nonjudicial activities they may legitimately engage in, for profit or not.

The final overarching norm of behavior that is applicable to judges is that of maintaining honor and dignity, as the French would say, or, in American terminology, not bringing disrepute upon the judiciary. These are rather open-ended requirements that can be applied to wholly personal behavior as well as to professional conduct. Such elastic terms have been applied to Western judiciaries both historically and contemporaneously, and they apparently relate to types of conduct that vary from country to country and from era to era.

The comportment expected of a judge in the Ancien Régime was behavior in a manner that was above reproach in both professional and private life. Abuse of office was officially prohibited, along with violations of what might be regarded as criminal law. Punishments for failings were severe, including exauctoration and, not infrequently, execution in some particularly demeaning fashion. Notably, the French during this era treated romantic passion as a mitigating circumstance that might save a judge from the most serious punishments. Specific expectations for English judges in the same time period are far less clear, but the record shows that judges were convicted by Parliament for bribery and corruption or were removed by the king for making politically undesirable decisions. Whatever gave offense to either the monarch or Parliament might place a judge in jeopardy. Again, the sanctions imposed were harsh; judges were executed, banished, or imprisoned for their failings.

The eighteenth and nineteenth centuries witnessed a shift in attitude, not about ethical norms of judicial behavior, but about the punishments that infractions entailed. "Good behavior" was introduced as the standard in England in 1701, and only one higher court judge has been found to have violated that requirement. The cases that Parliament has investigated thereafter suggest that a judge must have acted with corrupt motives to render any conduct as beyond good behavior.

The rather imprecise requirement of good behavior was also adopted as the standard for U.S. judges, although they may also be removed for treason, bribery, or high crimes and misdemeanors. None has ever been convicted by the Senate of either treason or bribery. High crimes and misdemeanors have been interpreted by both the House of Representatives and the Senate as including a wide scope of activities, ranging from personal corruption to adhering to the Confederacy and from blatant partisan bias to cheating on income taxes. Approximately equivalent and equally vague language has been adopted by the various American states. At the urging of the American Bar Association in the twentieth century, a more explicit code of conduct has been articulated. Conflict of interest, involvement with charities, appropriate forms of outside work, and the like have been considerably clarified, but there remains the overarching, nonspecific statement that a judge should in both public and private life avoid impropriety and the appearance of impropriety.

Judges in France were admonished as early as the Napoleonic era and throughout the rest of the nineteenth century to preserve the dignity and honor of the judicial office and to behave scrupulously. The obligation of political reserve that prohibited a judge from exhibiting any hostile attitude toward the government evolved during that time. Recognized professional faults were abuse of power, taking actions beyond the powers of the office, and offenses in the discharge of judicial duties. Along with a rather obvious proscription against criminal behavior, there were quite broad requirements relating to private behavior. All of these expectations about judicial conduct have been carried forward under the Fifth Republic.

Ethical requirements imposed on Italian judges under the republic are a virtual mirror image of those adopted by the French: maintaining the public image and prestige of the office, avoiding conflicts of interest, not abusing judicial powers, and not being absent without leave. The Italian innovation is the requirement that a judge may not live outside the assigned jurisdiction. More notable, though, is the absence of any requirement that even resembles the French obligation of political reserve. Italian magistrates engage actively in the nation's political discourse, and the various unions of magistrates make political inclinations strikingly apparent.

The limits of acceptable conduct are remarkably similar, with exceptions like living within one's jurisdiction or the ban on absence without leave. In France, Italy, and the United States the clear indication is that behavior that might not be illegal or even unacceptable for other people, including those holding other public offices, can be unethical for a judge. A lack of precision, however, in setting out what specific activities, short of criminal conduct, might run afoul of these ethics is likewise endemic to each of these systems. It is perhaps even more pronounced in England, where no judge has been removed or even formally sanctioned for conduct since 1830. The specific cases in the other countries in which judges have fallen short of expectations are so few in number that a canon of proscribed conduct that will result in punishment is not possible. A generalized appeal to the good sense and conscience of judges seemingly undergirds judicial ethics. All that is offered is something akin to the speeches at the Mercuriales in the Ancien Régime, or the broad admonitions of the constitutions of the Roman Empire or the republic that appeal to the judges' moral and ethical sensibilities. Concrete examples are wanting. Even so, if the number of cases that have been brought can be trusted as a measure of the ethicalness of the judiciary in all four countries, the lessons have been understood by the judges. Precious few have been caught in transgressions and punished.

Judicial Accountability

Processes for disciplining judges have not remained static over time but rather have evolved. Some changes have been dramatic, whereas others, such as what constitutes improper conduct, have simply made subtle shifts over time. The most stark turn has taken place in the moderation of punishment for erring judges. The death penalty was once imposed in both the Ancien Régime and in England, but removal from office has replaced it as the most severe punishment meted out. The humiliation that accompanies public censure or criminal liability when illegal behavior is uncovered is the sanction now used in all of our modern democracies.

There is, moreover, seemingly minimal accountability in our modern examples. Aggregate figures are not available because of the confidentiality that now shrouds many discipline processes and because of the discrepancies in counting, along with gaps in data on the number of voluntary retirements or resignations that result from disciplinary procedures or the number of complaints that are resolved informally. We know that in England no higher court judge has been removed since 1830, but there are clues that some have chosen retirement under pressure from their peers. Likewise, a mere handful of lower court judges have lost their offices at the hands of the lord chancellor.

Since the advent of the republic in Italy in 1948, removal has taken place only for improper business relationships, excessive indebtedness if related to gambling, mafia associations, or criminal charges. Though there have been many allegations, precious few have resulted in open removal. France under the Fifth Republic has similarly demonstrated a reluctance to remove magistrates. In the 63 cases of alleged misconduct through October of 1991, the most serious punishments were mandatory retirement with loss of pension and involuntary transfers.

The United States offers only a slight variation on those themes, particularly at the national level, where only seven judges have been removed from office through the impeachment procedure. The House of Representatives has, like the British House of Commons, investigated far more judges than it has removed. More than 50 investigations resulted in 13 resignations and 5 censures.[21] Parallel figures are not available on judges who may have resigned or retired as a consequence of investigations that began under the auspices of the Justice Department. A far greater number of state judges have been removed, many of them because of efforts of state judicial conduct organizations. There is no way of determining how many others were held accountable for their actions by the electorate.

The U.S. numbers of dismissals, which is far higher than in any of the other nations we have considered, does not necessarily indicate that America has produced an excessive number of indolent, corrupt, and negligent judges. The total number of judges largely accounts for the variations.

There are currently around 30,000 sitting judges in the United States, in contrast to a magistrature in Italy or in France of approximately 7,000 and a mere 1,000 high court judges in England. Even so, the number of judges who have been removed from office in all four nations is quite low, clearly pointing to emphasis on independence as a value over accountability.

Others have considered similar questions and reached inconclusive results. Guarnieri suggests that the most effective mechanisms for restraining judicial misbehavior are public opinion, judicial socialization, collegial courts, the appellate process, and self-restraint.[22] Since all of the means are informal, he sees an insurmountable tension between judicial power and democratic principles,[23] leading him to conclude that there is no solution that is optimal for democracies.[24] Public opinion is limited as a restraint on judges who are insulated by guarantees of independence, and judicial socialization is formalized only in France, in the ENM. Collegial courts predominate at the appellate level in all four systems, but only individual judges decide cases at the trial level in the United States and England. Appeals may correct errors in decisions of lower court judges, but are not particularly effective for exposing bias or corruption.

Cappelletti organizes discipline processes around the world into four types. The repressive model is that in which judges serve at the pleasure of the executive and therefore can be expected to act in accordance with executive wishes. The English model until the eighteenth century fits this description, as would judiciaries in various authoritarian regimes. His second category is the autonomous system, where judges are a *corps séparé*. Behavior is monitored by the corporation of judges, as was the case in the French Ancien Régime, where magistrates "became so deaf to societal needs as to turn into one of the most hated targets of the . . . Revolution."[25] The current French and Italian systems for monitoring judicial behavior are a modification of this model, with magistrates comprising a major part of their respective CSMs. The last model, and the one Cappelletti advocates, is the responsive system, in which magistrates are liable to the "consumers of law and government."[26]

A basic assumption underlying the analysis of both Guarnieri and Cappelletti, as well as those few democratic theorists who address the place of courts in democracies, is that judicial power is of the same nature everywhere. Of course, it is not. In England judges exercise no power of judicial review over acts of Parliament and have only a very circumscribed ability to confront the powers of the state. Judges merely "patrol the boundaries."[27] French magistrates are explicitly denied any power of judicial review, and separate administrative courts consider allegations of government abuse of power. Judges in both of these nations act on the periphery of political power.

The Italian magistrature's sphere of action is similarly restricted. Judicial review is the prerogative of a separate Constitutional Court, and ordinary judges act only as the butlers who admit questions to that body. Administrative courts consider questions of administrative or governmental missteps. What distinguishes Italian magistrates somewhat from their French brethren is a peculiar form of activism that characterizes some individual magistrates. They are the "assault judges," who "no longer separate politics and social issues from the laws but try to make a name for themselves by 'attacking' a situation, a problem, an institution or an individual."[28] This phenomenon is not endemic to the whole Italian judiciary, however, even though there have been specific situations, particularly in the battles against terrorism and against the mafia or in investigations of political corruption, when it seemed as though the judiciary were acting as a powerful, monolithic body. Italian magistrates are generally restricted to acting within a very limited sphere that excludes overt political power.

Only in the United States, where decentralized judicial review is practiced, is the judiciary a real political power that can directly affect the democratic process. The force of judicial power is most typically felt as a pressure that inhibits legislative or executive actions that are of questionable constitutionality. As it was conceived at both the national and the state level, the American judiciary acts as part of a triad of political power. A particular confluence of events permitted the U.S. courts "to emerge as a key participant in the national political process."[29]

Judges in Democracy

What does this say about the accountability of judges in democracies? First, we need to return to that rather generic definition of democracy provided by Dahl, which requires no more than the existence of "processes by which ordinary citizens exert a relatively high degree of control of leaders."[30] It requires, as Lawson added, that tenure in office is always temporary and conditional.[31] Accountability is not, however, the same for all offices; it must be conceived of as proportionate to power. Lesser accountability is consistent with little power, but greater accountability attaches to increased power. Judicial authority, though it cannot be totally separated from judicial status, legal culture, and the political environment, becomes the potent independent variable that molds monitoring mechanisms and ethical norms, that in turn determine judicial accountability.

This proportionality of authority to accountability is consistent with our findings about the systems for ensuring judicial accountability in the four democracies studied. French, Italian, and English judges cannot challenge the democratic authority of the state, and their accountability is less democratically maintained. The Italian system most closely resembles Cappelletti's "autonomous" model, but the corporation of judges cannot act without the concurrence of representatives of the political branches. The minister of justice, as a representative of the executive, is involved in the process, and notables named by a political branch are also represented in the system. The procedures are not democratic, but the political branches have influence.

The English system for monitoring the behavior of high court judges might be classified by Cappelletti as "responsive," since elected representatives in the House of Commons have half of the voice in the address procedure to remove judges. The term does not fit, however, when practice is closely considered. The system functions more along the lines of Cappelletti's "autonomous" model, since no judge has been removed by address of Parliament in almost 200 years. By contrast, the lower judiciary is policed, at least on the face of it, by a "repressive" system, whereby a representative of the executive, the lord chancellor, may dismiss a judge, and there is no appeal from that decision. The terminology seems a bit out of place, however, since very few judges have been dismissed in this fashion and none were removed for political reasons.

Judges in the United States hold, on the other hand, substantial political power, even if its potential for use is greater than the reality of its application. That power is balanced by "responsive" accountability, in that all judges may be removed either through some form of election—whether partisan, nonpartisan, or retention—or through actions of elected representatives in cases of impeachment or address. The apparent reluctance of representatives or electors to turn sitting judges out of office has led to the introduction of auxiliary agencies. The Judicial Conduct Act at the federal level created a kind of corporate model of judges monitoring the conduct of other judges, though removal from office remains exclusively in the hands of elected representatives. The states have adopted judicial conduct organizations, mixed bodies that serve as an adjunct to more responsive mechanisms.

When viewed in this light, the question of judicial accountability resolves itself into a dilemma of democracy that is not peculiar to the judicial branch. Indeed, judiciaries may be evaluated only in their larger institutional context. Publicly accountable judges would not render an otherwise authoritarian regime democratic. Nor does an unaccountable judiciary necessarily imply a nondemocratic government. The balance struck among the players determines the character of the state.

Gould argues, moreover, that there is an intrinsic contradiction between participation and authority in political life, for if participation is a central value, authority must be excluded.[32] Diamond discusses the same difficulty in deciding between plurality and majority electoral mechanisms; for him, the paradox is one of representativeness versus governability. The former requires that power be held accountable to popular control, which conflicts with the requirements for governability: sufficient concentration and autonomy of power.[33] For Dahrendorf, the question is the equilibrium between effectiveness and legitimacy.[34] In the parlance of law and judges, the issue is that of balancing independence with accountability. And, as Dahrendorf notes, the relationship is asymmetrical because a government may be effective without being legitimate, but "it is more difficult to imagine governments which are legitimate without being effective."[35] Sufficient independence must be accorded to judges to allow them to be effective; legitimacy, or accountability, is necessary but not necessarily as compelling.

Much of the criticism directed at contemporary courts is that they are ineffective—incapable of stemming the rising tide of crime, unable to dispatch ever-increasing civil litigation, and slow to react to changing societal values. This is but one side of the challenge to governability of modern democracies, which appear incapable of sustaining economic growth, integrating the flow of immigrants, or formulating coherent foreign policies in the post–cold war environment.

Some judges act corruptly, either personally or politically, and when that is exposed, the public reacts with indignation. Ethical lapses are no more commonplace in the judiciary than in the executive and legislative, but when a judge makes a misstep, it may "have damaging consequences far out of proportion to its intrinsic moral seriousness."[36] Unlike their counterparts in other government positions, judges are expected to have special technical education and intellectual expertise and also to adhere to exceptionally high moral standards. Requirements for judicial accountability or legitimacy may be be viewed most usefully as parallel to requirements for other policy-makers in democracies. Effectiveness or ability to govern is crucial to the maintenance of legitimacy. There are progressively more serious limitations on the effectiveness of democratic governments in satisfying rising expectations and absorbing changes in societal values. What is needed in a free society is "an unworried government, and that means one which is effective where necessary and legitimate throughout."[37]

Notes

Chapter One: Judges and Democracy

1. Dahl, *A Preface to Democratic Theory*, 3.
2. Rodotá, *La Corte Costituzionale*, 14–15.
3. Montesquieu, *The Spirit of the Laws*, 152.
4. Shapiro, *Courts*, 1 and 7.
5. Ibid., 20.
6. Becker, *Comparative Judicial Politics*, 13.
7. UN Commission on Human Rights, "Basic Principles on the Independence of the Judiciary."
8. Dubois, *From Ballot to Bench*, 3–20.
9. Mény, *Government and Politics in Western Europe*, 324.
10. As quoted in Morton, "Judicial Activism in France," 134.
11. Ely, *Democracy and Distrust*, 1.
12. McDowell, "The Moral Wish as Father to Constitutional Thought," 832.
13. Alexander, "Of Two Minds about Law and Minds," 2447.
14. Perry, *The Constitution, the Courts and Human Rights*, 11.
15. Sherry, "Issue Manipulation by the Burger Court," 612.
16. Tushnet, *Red, White and Blue*, 3.
17. Mény, *Government and Politics*, 298.
18. Abraham, *The Judicial Process*, 291.
19. Berger, *Congress v. the Supreme Court*, 184.
20. Dahl, "Decision-Making in a Democracy," 275.
21. Preuss, "Aus dem Geiste des Konsenses," 1–12.

22. Mandel, *The Charter of Rights,* 42.

23. Volcansek and Lafon, *Judicial Selection,* 11–12.

24. Blondel, *Comparative Government,* 323.

25. Shapiro, *Courts,* 28.

26. Frank, *Courts on Trial,* 295.

27. Ibid., 293.

28. Blackstone, "Parliamentary Omnipotence (1765)," 39.

29. Bagehot, *The English Constitution,* 201.

30. As quoted in Plucknett, *Studies in English Legal History* 14:34.

31. Waltman, "Judicial Activism in England," 35.

32. Drewry, "Judicial Politics in Britain," 12.

33. Devlin, *The Judge,* 2.

34. Drewry, "Judicial Politics in Britain," 19.

35. Ibid., 25.

36. Baar, "Judicial Activism in Canada," 54.

37. Mandel, *Charter of Rights,* 5.

38. Ibid., 61.

39. Galligan, "Judicial Activism in Australia," 70.

40. Galligan and Slater, "Judicial Intrusion into the Australian Cabinet."

41. Dhavan, "Judicializing Politics: Indian Incongruities," 10.

42. Ibid., 34.

43. Shapiro, "The Juridicalization of Politics in the United States," 101.

44. Baum, *American Courts,* 6–7.

45. Damaska, *The Faces of Justice and State Authority,* 37.

46. Lafon, "La Judicialisation de la Politique en France," 136.

47. Shapiro, *Courts,* 134.

48. Lafon, "La Judicialisation de la Politique en France," 137.

49. Van Koppen, "Judicial Policy-Making in the Netherlands," 80–92.

50. Verougstraete, "Judicial Politics in Belgium," 93–108.

51. Tate, "Courts and Crisis Regimes," 311–38.

52. Shapiro, *Courts,* 65.

53. Blondel, *Comparative Government,* 325.

54. Schmidhauser, "Introduction: The Impact of Political Change upon Law, Courts and Judicial Elites," 231.

55. Becker, *Comparative Judicial Politics,* 144.

56. Gamarra, *The System of Justice in Bolivia,* 86–87.

57. Kommers, *The Constitutional Jurisprudence of the Federal Republic of Germany,* 25.

58. Landfried, "Judicial Policy-Making in Germany," 59.

59. Stone, *The Birth of Judicial Politics in France,* 50.

60. Blondel, *Comparative Government,* 328; and Shapiro, *Courts,* 24.

61. Belloni, "The Labour Community and the British Judiciary," 81.

62. Becker, *Comparative Judicial Politics*, 163.

63. Lafon, "The Judicial Career in France," 101.

64. Volcansek, "The Judicial Role in Italy," 324.

65. Royer, *La Société Judiciare depuis le xviii Siècle*, 292.

66. *Hastings v. Judicial Conference of the United States*, 593 F. Supp. 1371 (1984), at 1383.

67. Dahl, *A Preface to Democratic Theory*, 3.

68. Schmitter and Karl, "What Democracy Is . . . and Is Not," 40.

69. Olson, "Dictatorship, Democracy, and Development," 572.

70. Sartori, *The Theory of Democracy Revisited*, 30.

71. Whitehead, "International Aspects of Democratization," 8.

72. Sartori, *Theory of Democracy*, 33.

73. Lijphart, *Democracies*, 191–93.

74. See, for example, Bermeo, "Rethinking Regime Change," 359–77; and Gillespie, "Democratic Consolidation in the Southern Cone," 92–113.

75. Lawson, "Conceptual Issues in the Comparative Study of Regime Change and Democratization," 183–205.

76. Przeworski, "Some Problems in the Study of the Transition to Democracy," 60.

77. Note the absence of any mention of the terms in early works, such as Downs, *An Economic Theory of Democracy*, or in the more recent, Putnam, *Making Democracy Work*.

78. Diamond, "Three Paradoxes of Democracy," 96.

79. Marsh and Olsen, "The New Institutionalism," 734–49.

80. Skocpol, *Vision and Method in Historical Sociology*, 4.

81. March and Olsen, "New Institutionalism," 734.

82. Sangmpam, "The Overpoliticized State and Democratization," 415.

83. Linz and Stepan, eds., *The Breakdown of Democratic Regimes*, 69.

84. Sartori, *Theory of Democracy*, 326.

85. Bobbio, *The Future of Democracy*, 143.

86. Dahl, *Democracy and Its Critics*, 177.

87. Ibid., 187–88.

88. Ibid., 187–91.

89. Guarnieri, *Magistratura e Politica in Italia*, 27–37.

90. Ibid., 38–39.

91. Ibid., 40–41.

92. Sartori, *Theory of Democracy*, 245.

93. Lawson, "Conceptual Issues," 189.

94. Cappelletti, "'Who Watches the Watchmen?' " 18.

95. See, for example, Holland, ed., *Judicial Activism in Comparative Perspective;* Jackson and Tate, eds., *Comparative Judicial Review and Public Policy;* and Volcansek, ed., *Judicial Politics and Policy-Making in Western Europe*.

96. Manheim and Rich, *Empirical Political Analysis*, 217.

97. Mahler, *Comparative Politics*, 150.

98. Schmidhauser, "Alternative Conceptual Frameworks in Comparative Cross-National Legal and Judicial Research," 35.

99. Sartori, "Concept Misinformation in Comparative Politics," 1039.

100. Ibid., 1052.

101. Lijphart, "Comparative Politics and the Comparative Method," 685.

102. Lijphart, "The Comparable-Cases Strategy in Comparative Research," 159.

103. Ibid., 164.

104. See, for a complete exposition of these problems, Przeworski and Teune, *The Logic of Comparative Social Inquiry;* and Ragin, *The Comparative Method.*

105. Smith, "Political Jurisprudence," 102.

106. Ibid., 101–3.

107. Lijphart, "The Comparable-Cases Strategy," 172–73.

108. Ibid., p. 159.

109. Lipset, *Political Man*, 64.

110. Dahrendorf, "Effectiveness and Legitimacy," 397.

Chapter Two: France

1. Abraham, *The Judicial Process*, 267.

2. Volcansek and Lafon, *Judicial Selection*, 43–44, 55–57, and 99–100.

3. Royer, *La société judiciaire*, 292.

4. Volcansek and Lafon, *Judicial Selection*, 58–67.

5. For all cases discussed in this section, see Rousselet, *Histoire de la Magistrature Française* 2:38–39, 179–91.

6. Volcansek and Lafon, *Judicial Selection*, 115 and 120–21.

7. Royer, *Société judiciaire*, 290–91.

8. The cases cited are extracted from Rousselet, *Histoire de la Magistrature* 2:185–86, 200–201; and Royer, *Société judiciaire*, 290–93.

9. Volcansek and Lafon, *Judicial Selection*, 120.

10. Lafon, "The Judicial Career in France," 102.

Chapter Three: Italy

1. Micali, "Per un Contributo," 4:145–49.

2. Negri, *Il Quadro Costitutionale*, 24–25.

3. Senese, "La Formazione dei Magistrati," 5:538.

4. Guarnieri, *Magistratura e Politica*, 83–84.

5. Senese, "Il Governo della Magistratura," 21.

6. Guarnieri, *Magistratura e Politica*, 84.

7. Senese, "Il Governo della Magistratura," 21–22.

8. Guarnieri, *Magistratura e Politica*, 86–87.

9. R. D. Lgt. No. 511, 31 May 1946.

10. D. Lgt. C.P.S. No. 264, 13 September 1946.

11. Senese, "Il Governo della Magistratura," 22.

12. Ehrmann, *Comparative Legal Cultures,* 77.

13. Cicconetti, Cortese, Torcolini, and Traversa, *La Costituzione della Repubblica* 6:245–46.

14. Pizzorusso, *Sistema Istituzionale,* 282–83.

15. Tesauro, *Manuale di Diritto Pubblico,* 438–39; and Bartole, "Il Potere Giudiziario," 642–46.

16. Valentino, *Il Presidente della Repubblica,* 85.

17. Carbone, "Art. 110," 87.

18. Constitutional Court, Judgment no. 168, 23 December 1963.

19. Constitutional Court, Judgment no. 2, 14 March 1968.

20. Constitutional Court, Judgment no. 379, 27 July 1992.

21. Law no. 195, 24 March 1958.

22. Guarnieri, *Magistratura e Politica,* 94–95.

23. Hine, *Governing Italy,* 68.

24. La Palombara, *Democracy Italian Style,* 77.

25. Pizzorusso, *Sistema Istituzionale,* 280.

26. Pizzorusso, "Poteri del CSM," 727.

27. Constitutional Court, Judgment no. 12, 19 January 1971.

28. Constitutional Court, Judgment no. 44, 14 May 1968.

29. Crisafulli and Paladin, *Commentario Breve,* 663.

30. Ordine Giudiziario, Article 12.

31. R.D. Lgt. no. 511, 31 May 1946.

32. Coen, "La Responsabilità Disciplinare," IV, 384.

33. Law no. 1, 3 January 1981.

34. R.D. Lgt no. 511, 31 May 1946, Article 19.

35. De Franciscis, "Italy," 164; and Di Federico, "The Italian Judicial Profession," 54.

36. Consiglio Superiore della Magistratura, *La Responsabilità Disciplinare dei Magistrati,* 45.

37. Di Federico, "La Selezione dei Magistrati," 16–21.

38. Ibid., 49.

39. Unpublished data were made available by the Ufficio Studi del CSM.

40. Quaderni del Consiglio Superiore della Magistratura, *Manuale dell'Udienza Disciplinare,* 40.

41. Ibid., 51.

42. Ibid., 59.

43. Senese, "Il Governo della Magistratura," 27–28.

44. D.P.R. no. 89., 12 April 1976.

45. Law no. 74, 12 April 1990.

46. Constitutional Court, Judgment no. 29, 16 January 1987.

47. Volcansek, "The Judicial Role," 322.

48. Law no. 117, 13 April 1988.

49. Constitutional Court, Judgment no. 468, 22 October 1990.

50. De Palo, "Sulla Responsabilità dei Giudici," IV, 399.

51. Negri, *Quadro Costitutionale*, 173.

52. Borré, "Indipendenza e Politicità," 151.

53. Guarnieri, *Magistratura e Politica*, 95–102.

54. Palazzolo, "Composizione ed Elezione," IV, 166.

55. "I Giudici Piacciono Tre Volte Tanto," 16.

56. Borré, "Indipendenza e Politicità," 149.

57. Ibid.

58. "Carnevale a Mezzo Stipendio," 20.

59. "Azione Disciplinare per i Giudici Massoni," 7.

60. "Quaranta Giudici sotto Inchiesta," 8.

61. "Magistratopoli," 5.

62. Chamber of Deputies, Parliamentary Acts (Doc.I, N.9). Message to the Chambers by the President of the Republic, appended by the Report of the Presidential Committee for the study of the problems related to the laws and to the functions of the CSM, of 6 February 1991 (also known as *Relazione Paladin*).

Chapter Four: England

1. Wade and Phillips, *Constitutional Law*, 30.

2. As quoted in A.H. Manchester, *Modern Legal History*, 82.

3. Blackstone, *Commentaries on the Laws of England* 4:139.

4. Pannick, *Judges*, 88–89.

5. Babington, *The Rule of Law in Britain*, xii-xiii; and Curzon, *English Legal History*, 208–9.

6. Babington, *Rule of Law in Britain*, 72.

7. Roskell, *The Impeachment of Michael de la Pole*, 194.

8. Plucknett, *Studies in English Legal History*, 10:145–47.

9. Babington, *Rule of Law in Britain*, 99.

10. Kiralfy, *Potter's Historical Introduction to English Law*, 145.

11. Kenyon, *The Stuart Constitution*, 75.

12. Curzon, *English Legal History*, 210.

13. Kenyon, *The Stuart Constitution*, 77.

14. Shetreet, *Judges on Trial*, 127.

15. Kenyon, *The Stuart Constitution*, 89–90.

16. Babington, *Rule of Law in Britain*, 147–48.

17. As quoted in Kenyon, *The Stuart Constitution*, 101.

18. Shetreet, *Judges on Trial*, 127.

19. Kenyon, *The Stuart Constitution*, 397.

20. Ibid., 399.

21. Curzon, *English Legal History*, 210.

22. Kenyon, *The Stuart Constitution*, 395; and Shetreet, *Judges on Trial*, 127.

23. Kenyon, *The Stuart Constitution*, 396–97.

24. Curzon, *English Legal History*, 210.

25. II Will.3 c. 11.

26. Notes from the Earl of Hardwicke's speech, reported in 1 Geo. III, 1008–10.

27. Shetreet, *Judges on Trial*, 129.

28. 1 Geo. III, 1007.

29. Ibid.

30. Holdsworth, *A History of English Law*, 385.

31. Shetreet, *Judges on Trial*, 143.

32. Babington, *Rule of Law in Britain*, 235–37.

33. Jewell, *British Constitution*, 171.

34. Stevens, *Law and Politics*, 101.

35. 39 and 40 Vict. c. 59.

36. Cecil, *The English Judge*, 50.

37. Brazier, "Judicial Immunity and the Independence of the Judiciary," 401.

38. Blackstone, *Commentaries on the Laws of England*, 1:258.

39. Wade and Phillips, *Constitutional Law*, 308.

40. Alder, *Constitutional and Administrative Law*, 268.

41. Pannick, *Judges*, 91–92.

42. The following instances of address are taken from Shetreet, *Judges on Trial*, 139–51.

43. Wade and Phillips, *Constitutional Law*, 308; and Shetreet, *Judges on Trial*, 130.

44. Pannick, *Judges*, 87.

45. Supreme Court Act of 1981, c. 54.

46. Courts and Legal Service Act 1990, c. 41.

47. Supreme Court Act of 1981, c. 54.

48. Phillips and Hudson, *O. Hood Phillips' First Book of English Law*, 32–33.

49. Griffith, *The Politics of the Judiciary*, 23–34.

50. Pannick, *Judges*, 91.

51. *Parliamentary Debates* (Commons), V. 200 (19 May 1992), 93–4w.

52. M. Brazier, "Judicial Immunity," 418.

53. (1612) 10 Co Rep 68 b.

54. *Hamond v. Howell*, (1674) 1 Mod Rep. 119.

55. Curzon, *English Legal History*, 210.

56. As quoted in Alder, *Constitutional and Administrative Law*, 183.

57. *Sirros v. Moore* (1974), 3 All ER 776, 782.

58. Ibid., 785.

59. (1985) A.C. 528.

60. Boswell, *Life of Johnson*, 619.

61. Cecil, *The English Judge*, 50.

62. As quoted in Manchester, *Modern Legal History,* 83.

63. R. Brazier, *Constitutional Reform,* 152.

64. Griffith, *Politics of the Judiciary,* 35.

65. Tate, "Recruitment to the British Appellate Judiciary," 263–64.

66. *Parliamentary Debates* (Commons), V. 178 (29 October 1990), 353w.

67. *Parliamentary Debates* (Commons), V. 203 (2 March 1992), 40w.

68. *Parliamentary Debates* (Commons), V. 209 (19 June 1992), 680w.

69. Darnton, "England's Judges," A19.

70. *Judicial Appointments.*

71. Courts and Legal Services Act of 1990, c. 41.

72. Shetreet, *Judges on Trial,* 410.

73. R. Brazier, *Constitutional Reform,* 156.

74. Ibid., 157.

Chapter 5: United States

1. Canon, "Commentary on State Selection of Judges," 748.

2. Warrick, *Judicial Selection in the United States,* 9–15.

3. Council of State Governments, *The Book of the States, 1992–93,* 233–35.

4. *Bradley v. Fisher,* 80 U.S. 335 (1871).

5. *Pulliam v. Allen,* 466 U.S. 522 (1984).

6. Hamilton, *Federalist No. 78,* 503.

7. Ibid., 505.

8. Hamilton, *Federalist No. 79,* 514.

9. Hamilton, *Federalist No. 65,* 423–24.

10. Johnson, *Foundations of Power,* 209.

11. Turner, "The Impeachment of John Pickering," 487–88.

12. Ellis, *The Jeffersonian Crisis,* 69–70.

13. Ibid., 488.

14. *The Trial of John Pickering,* S. Doc. 876, 20–21.

15. Ellis, *The Jeffersonian Crisis,* 96.

16. Turner, "The Impeachment of John Pickering," 496–98.

17. Ibid., 505.

18. Rehnquist, *Grand Inquests,* 130.

19. Berger, *Impeachment,* 226.

20. Dilliard, "Samuel Chase," 1:188–89.

21. Corwin, "Samuel Chase," 36.

22. Dilliard, "Samuel Chase," 1:193–95.

23. Chase, "Charge to Grand Jury (1803)," 1:192–94.

24. As quoted in Lillich, "The Chase Impeachment," 51.

25. Baker, *John Marshall,* 427.

26. Lillich, "The Chase Impeachment," 64.

27. *Trial of Samuel Chase,* 5–8.

28. Ellis, *The Jeffersonian Crisis,* 98; Baker, *John Marshall,* 430; and Lillich, "The Chase Impeachment," 64.

29. *Trial of Samuel Chase,* 2:493.

30. Lillich, "The Chase Impeachment," 71.

31. Dumbauld, *Thomas Jefferson and the Law,* 35.

32. Dilliard, "Samuel Chase," 197.

33. *Journal of the House of Representatives,* 7 January 1830, 591–96.

34. *Proceedings of the Senate,* Appendix, Preliminary to the Trial of the Impeachment of James H. Peck, Judge of the District Court of the United States for the District of Missouri, 26 April 1830 to 31 January 1831, 238–326.

35. *Journal of the House of Representatives,* 9 May 1862, 709–12.

36. *Journal of the Senate,* Appendix, Executive Proceedings of the Senate, from which the Injunction of Secrecy Has Been Removed during the Second Session of the Thirty-seventh Congress, 26 June 1862, 895–904.

37. Van Tassel, *Why Judges Resign,* 20.

38. Borkin, *The Corrupt Judge,* 219–58.

39. Ten Broek, "Partisan Politics and Federal Judgeship Impeachment Since 1903," 185.

40. Ibid.

41. *Proceedings in the Senate Preliminary to the Trial of Charles Swayne, Judge of the District Court of the United States in and for the Northern District of Florida, upon the Articles of Impeachment Exhibited by the House of Representatives* (Washington, D.C.: U.S. Government Printing Office, 1905), 583–94.

42. Ten Broek, "Partisan Politics," 186–88.

43. *Articles of Impeachment Presented against Robert W. Archbald* (Washington, D.C.: U.S. Government Printing Office, 1912).

44. Ten Broek, "Partisan Politics," 190–92.

45. Ibid., 194–95.

46. *Journal of the House of Representatives,* 24 February 1933, 303–5.

47. *Journal of the Senate,* 24 May 1933, 338–44.

48. *Journal of the Senate,* 10 March 1936, 473–77.

49. *Journal of the Senate,* 17 April 1936, 506–12.

50. *U.S. v. Isaacs and Kerner,* 493 Fed.2d 1124, 1142.

51. Ibid., 1144.

52. Murphy, *Fortas,* 566.

53. Volcansek, *Judicial Impeachment,* 36–43.

54. *Congressional Record,* 9 October 1986, S-15759–62.

55. Volcansek, *Judicial Impeachment,* 68–116.

56. Ibid., 120–51.

57. Bermant, Schwarzer, Sussman, and Wheeler, *Imposing a Moratorium on the Number of Federal Judges,* 3.

58. Blackstone, *Commentaries on the Laws of England,* 4:121–22.

59. Black, *Impeachment: A Handbook,* 39–40.

60. Fenton, "The Scope of the Impeachment Power," 745.

61. Gerhardt, "The Constitutional Limits to Impeachment and Its Alternatives," 88.

62. Morgan, "The Appearance of Propriety, " 597.

63. Ibid., 597–98.

64. American Bar Association, *Canons of Judicial Ethics, 1924,* Canon 4.

65. American Bar Association, *Canons of Judicial Ethics, 1972,* Canon 2.

66. Lubet, "Participation by Judges in Civic and Charitable Activities," 69.

67. Shaman, Lubet, and Alfini, "The 1990 Code of Judicial Conduct," 21.

68. Volcansek, "Codes of Judicial Ethics," 505.

69. Rehnquist, "Sense and Nonsense about Judicial Ethics," 696.

70. O'Connor and Henze, *"During Good Behavior,"* 17.

71. *LaBuy v. Howes Leather Company,* 325 U.S. 249 (1956).

72. P.L. 96–458, 94 *Stat.* 2035 (1980).

73. Data were compiled from the *Annual Report of the Director of the Administrative Office of the United States Courts,* from 1982 through 1990.

74. Fitzpatrick, "Misconduct and Disability of Federal Judges," 283.

75. Edwards, "Judicial Misconduct and Politics in the Federal System," 1080–81.

76. Flanders, "Judicial Discipline, Criminal Prosecution and Impeachment," 397–98.

77. Wood, *The Creation of the American Republic,* 16.

78. Dubois, *From Ballot to Bench,* 3.

79. Volcansek and Lafon, *Judicial Selection,* 76.

80. Coyle, "Judicial Selection and Tenure in Mississippi," 90.

81. Volcansek and Lafon, *Judicial Selection,* 91.

82. Baum, *American Courts,* 102.

83. Baum, "The Electoral Fates of Incumbent Judges," 424.

84. Dubois, "Voting Cues in Nonpartisan Trial Court Elections," 423.

85. Hojnacki and Baum, "Choosing Judicial Candidates," 300.

86. Lovrich, Pierce and Sheldon, "Citizen Knowledge and Voting in Judicial Elections," 33.

87. Dubois, "Voting Cues," 432.

88. McFadden, *Electing Justice,* 10.

89. Dubois, "Financing Trial Court Elections," 15.

90. Nicholson and Weiss, "Funding Judicial Campaigns in the Circuit Court of Cook County," 23.

91. Moog, "Campaign Financing for North Carolina's Appellate Courts," 75.

92. Alfini and Brooks, "Ethical Constraints on Judicial Election Campaigns," 671–722.

93. Jackson and Riddlesperger, "Money and Politics in Judicial Elections," 189.

94. Dubois, *From Ballot to Bench,* 94.

95. Smith and Garmel, "Judicial Election and Selection Procedures Challenged under the Voting Rights Act," 154–56.

96. Kales, *Unpopular Government in the United States,* chap. 7.

97. Carbon, "Judicial Retention Elections," 221.

98. Griffin and Horan, "Patterns of Voting Behavior in Judicial Retention Elections," 77.

99. Hall and Aspin, "What Twenty Years of Judicial Retention Elections Have Told Us," 344.

100. Carbon, "Judicial Retention Elections," 212.

101. Hall and Aspin, "Twenty Years of Judicial Retention Elections," 347.

102. Perlstein and Goldman, "Judicial Disciplinary Commissions," 93–95; and Rosenbaum, *Practices and Procedures of State Judicial Conduct Organizations,* xi.

103. Comisky and Patterson, *The Judiciary,* 156–65.

104. Lubet, *Beyond Reproach,* vii.

105. Ibid., 5.

106. Baum, *American Courts,* 161–62.

107. Carp and Stidham, *Judicial Process in America,* 268–69.

108. Miller, "Assessing the Functions of Judicial Conduct Organizations," 19.

109. Gardiner, "Preventing Judicial Misconduct," 114.

110. Rosenbaum, *Practices and Procedures of State Judicial Conduct Organizations,* 10.

111. Hoelzel, "No Easy Answers," 280.

112. Figures provided by Cindy Gray, director of the Center for Judicial Conduct Organizations, 27 July 1993 (Chicago, Ill.: American Judicature Society).

Chapter 6: Judging the Judges

1. "Mob Prosecutor to Aid in Inquiry," Y-10.

2. Schemo, "Seeking Leniency, Wachtler Blames Adversaries," Y-15.

3. "CSM: La Carriera Finità e Uno Stipendio Ridotto," 3.

4. "Sí, il CSM Ha Tollerato Inefficienze e Timidezze," 12.

5. Atkins, "Judicial Selection in Context," 580.

6. Grossman and Sarat, "Political Culture and Judicial Research," 192.

7. Volcansek and Lafon, *Judicial Selection,* 46.

8. Ibid., 120.

9. Aberbach, Putnam, and Rockman, *Bureaucrats and Politicians in Western Democracies,* 51–53.

10. Griffith, *The Politics of the Judiciary,* 23.

11. Ibid., 30–31.

12. Yackle, "Choosing Judges the Democratic Way," 317–27.

13. Kiser and Barzel, "The Origins of Democracy in England," 398.

14. Ibid., 399.

15. Abraham, *The Judicial Process,* 293.

16. Chemerinsky, "Evaluating Judicial Candidates," 1986.

17. Cappelletti, " 'Who Watches the Watchmen?' " 31.

18. Law no. 72–626.

19. Cappellcttti, " 'Who Watches the Watchmen?' " 48.

20. Berg, Hahn, and Schmidhauser, *Corruption in the American Political System,* 3.

21. Van Tassel, *Why Judges Resign,* 23.

22. Guarnieri, *Magistratura e Politica in Italia,* 38–39.

23. Ibid., 36.

24. Ibid., 40.

25. Cappelletti, " 'Who Watches the Watchmen?' " 60.

26. Ibid., 61.

27. Drewry, "Judicial Politics in Britain," 9.

28. De Franciscis, "Italy," 163.

29. Atkins, "Judicial Selection in Context," 581.

30. Dahl, *Preface to Democratic Theory,* 3.

31. Lawson, "Conceptual Issues in the Comparative Study of Regime Change and Democratization," 189.

32. Gould, *Rethinking Democracy,* 215.

33. Diamond, "Three Paradoxes of Democracy," 100–101.

34. Dahrendorf, "Effectiveness and Legitimacy," 398.

35. Ibid.

36. Braithwaite, *Who Judges the Judges?* 9.

37. Dahrendorf, "Effectiveness and Legitimacy," 410.

Bibliography

Aberbach, Joel D., Robert Putnam, and Bert A. Rockman. *Bureaucrats and Politicians in Western Democracies.* Cambridge: Harvard University Press, 1981.

Abraham, Henry J. *The Judicial Process.* New York: Oxford University Press, 1986.

Alder, John. *Constitutional and Administrative Law.* London: Macmillan, 1989.

Alexander, Larry. "Of Two Minds about Law and Minds." *Michigan Law Review* 88 (August 1990): 2444–49.

Alfini, James J., and Terrence J. Brooks. "Ethical Constraints on Judicial Election Campaigns: A Review and Critique of Canon 7." *Kentucky Law Journal* 77 (1989): 671–722.

Amato, Giuliano, and Augusto Barbera, eds. *Manuale di Diritto Pubblico* (Manual of public law). Bologna: Il Mulino, 1984.

American Bar Association. *Canons of Judicial Ethics.* Chicago: American Bar Association, 1924, 1972, 1990.

Annual Report of the Director of the Administrative Office of the United States Courts. Washington: U.S. Government Printing Office, 1982–91.

Articles of Impeachment Presented against Robert W. Archbald. Washington: U.S. Government Printing Office, 1912.

Atkins, Burton. "Judicial Selection in Context: The American and English Experience." *Kentucky Law Journal* 1988 (1988): 577–617.

"Azione Disciplinare per i Giudici Massoni" (Disciplinary action for the Masonic judges). *Il Tempo,* 22 June 1993: 7.

Baar, Carl. "Judicial Activism in Canada." In *Judicial Activism in Comparative Perspective,* ed. Kenneth M. Holland, 53–69. London: Macmillan, 1991.

Babington, Anthony. *The Rule of Law in Britain: From the Roman Occupation to the Present.* Chichester: Barry Rose Publishers, 1978.

Bagehot, Walter. *The English Constitution.* Oxford: Oxford University Press, 1877.

Baker, Leonard. *John Marshall: A Life in the Law.* New York: Macmillan Publishing Co., 1974.

Bartole, Sergio. "Il Potere Giudiziario" (The judicial power). In *Manual di Dirritto Pubblico,* ed. Giuliano Amato and Augusto Barbera, 642–46. Bologna: Il Mulino, 1984.

Baum, Lawrence. *American Courts: Process and Policy.* Boston: Houghton Mifflin Company, 1990.

———. "The Electoral Fates of Incumbent Judges in the Ohio Court of Common Pleas." *Judicature* 66 (April 1983): 420–30.

Becker, Theodore L. *Comparative Judicial Politics: The Political Functionings of Courts.* Chicago: Rand McNally and Company, 1970.

Belloni, Frank. "The Labour Community and the British Judiciary." *International Political Science Review* 13 (July 1992): 269–84.

Berg, Larry L., Harlan Hahn, and John R. Schmidhauser. *Corruption in the American Political System.* Morristown, N.J.: General Learning Press, 1976.

Berger, Raoul. *Congress v. the Supreme Court.* Cambridge: Harvard University Press, 1969.

———. *Impeachment: The Constitutional Problems.* Cambridge: Harvard University Press, 1974.

———. "Impeachment for 'High Crimes and Misdemeanors.' " *Southern California Law Review* 44 (Winter 1971): 395–460.

Bermant, Gordon, William W. Schwarzer, Edward Sussman, and Russell R. Wheeler. *Imposing a Moratorium on the Number of Federal Judges: Analysis of Arguments and Implications.* Washington: Federal Judicial Center, 1993.

Bermeo, Nancy. "Rethinking Regime Change." *Comparative Politics* 22 (April 1990): 359–77.

Black, Charles L. *Impeachment: A Handbook.* New Haven: Yale University Press, 1974.

Blackstone, William. *Commentaries on the Laws of England.* 4 vols. Oxford: Clarendon Press, 1778.

Blondel, Jean. *Comparative Government.* New York: Philip Allan, 1990.

Bobbio, Norberto. *The Future of Democracy.* Trans. Roger Griffin. Minneapolis: University of Minnesota Press, 1987.

Borkin, Joseph. *The Corrupt Judge: An Inquiry into Bribery and Other High Crimes and Misdemeanors in the Federal Courts.* New York: Clarkson N. Potter, Inc., 1962.

Borré, Giuseppe. "Indipendenza e Politicità della Magistratura" (Independence and politics of the magistrature). In *Governo e Autogoverno della Magistratura nell'Europa Occidentale,* ed. Pier Luigi Zanchetta, 145–52. Milan: Franco Agnelli, 1987.

Boswell, James. *Life of Johnson.* London: Oxford University Press, 1961.

Braithwaite, William Thomas. *Who Judges the Judges?* Chicago: American Bar Foundation, 1971.

Brazier, Margaret. "Judicial Immunity and the Independence of the Judiciary." *Public Law* (1976): 401–20.

Brazier, Rodney. *Constitutional Reform: Re-shaping the British Political System.* Oxford: Clarendon Press, 1991.

Canon, Bradley C. "Commentary on State Selection of Judges." *Kentucky Law Journal* 77 (1989): 747–57.

Cappelletti, Mauro. " 'Who Watches the Watchmen?' " *American Journal of Comparative Law* 31 (1983): 1–62.

Carbon, Susan B. "Judicial Retention Elections: Are They Serving Their Intended Purpose?" *Judicature* 64 (November 1980): 210–33.

Carbone, Vincenzo. "Art. 110." In *Commentario della Costituzione: Art. 108–110* (Commentary on the constitution: articles 108–110), ed. A. Pizzorusso, V. Zagrebelsky, and V. Carbone, 70–144. Bologna: Zanichelli Editore, 1992.

"Carnevale a Mezzo Stipendio" (Carnevale at half-salary). *La Repubblica,* 24 April 1993, 20.

Carp, Robert A., and Ronald Stidham. *Judicial Process in America.* Washington: CQ Press, 1993.

Cecil, Henry. *The English Judge.* London: Stevens and Sons, 1970.

Chase, Samuel. "Charge to Grand Jury (1803)." In *Documents of American Constitutional and Legal History,* 2 vols., ed. Melvin I. Urofsky, 1:192–94. New York: Alfred A. Knopf, 1989.

Chemerinsky, Erwin. "Evaluating Judicial Candidates." *Southern California Law Review* (September 1988): 1985–94.

Cicconetti, Stefano Maria, Maurizio Cortese, Giuseppe Torcolini, and Silvio Traversa, eds. *La Costituzione della Repubblica: Nei Lavori Preparatori della Assemblea Costituente* (The constitution of the Republic: the preparatory work of the Constituent Assembly). 8 vols. Rome: Camera dei Deputati, 1970.

Coen, Leopoldo. "La Responsibilità Disciplinare dei Magistrati: Ipotesi Ricostruttive e Problemi Applicativi" (The responsibility for discipline of the magistrates: reconstructive hypotheses and applicable problems). *Giurisprudenza Italiana* 143, pt. 4 (October 1991): 384.

Comisky, Marvin, and Philip C. Patterson. *The Judiciary—Selection, Compensation, Ethics and Discipline.* New York: Quorum Books, 1987.

Consiglio Superiore della Magistratura. *La Responsabilità Disciplinare dei Magistrati* (The responsibility for discipline of the magistrates), 2:45. Rome, 1976.

Corwin, Eward S. "Samuel Chase." In *Dictionary of American Biography,* ed. Allen Johnson and Dumas Malone, 36. New York: Charles Scribner's Sons, 1930.

Council of State Governments. *Book of the States, 1992–1993.* Lexington, Ky.: Council on State Governments, 1992.

Coyle, Arlen B. "Judicial Selection and Tenure in Mississippi." *Mississippi Law Journal* 43 (1972): 90–98.

Crisafulli, Vezio, and Livio Paladin. *Commentario Breve all Costituzione* (Brief commentary on the constitution). Padua: CEDAM, 1990.

"CSM: La Carriera Finità e Uno Stipendio Ridotto" (CSM: the career is over and the salary reduced). *Corriere della Sera,* 5 September 1993, 3.

Curzon, L. B. *English Legal History.* Plymouth, Mass.: MacDonald and Evans, 1979.

Dahl, Robert. "Decision-Making in a Democracy: The Supreme Court as a National Policy-Maker." *Journal of Public Law* 6 (Fall 1957): 275–85.

———. *Democracy and Its Critics.* New Haven: Yale University Press, 1989.

———. *A Preface to Democratic Theory.* Chicago: University of Chicago Press, 1956.

Dahrendorf, Ralf. "Effectiveness and Legitimacy: On the 'Governability' of Democracies." *Political Quarterly* 51 (October-December 1980): 393–410.

Damaska, Mirjan R. *The Faces of Justice and State Authority.* New Haven: Yale University Press, 1986.

D'Amato, Anthony. "Self-Regulation of Judicial Misconduct Could Be Mis-regulation." *Michigan Law Review* 89 (December 1990): 609–796.

Darnton, John. "England's Judges (and Hiring System) under Fire." *New York Times,* 18 July 1993, A19.

De Franciscis, Maria Elisabetta. "Italy." In *Legal Traditions and Systems,* ed. Alan N. Katz, 155–68. New York: Greenwood Press, 1986.

De Palo, Lucia Alessandra. "Sulla Responsabilità dei Giudici: Il Regime Transitorio" (Judicial responsibililty: the transitional regime). *Giurisprudenza Italiana* 143, pt. 4 (October 1991): 399.

Devlin, Patrick. *The Judge.* Oxford: Oxford University Press, 1979.

Dhavan, Rajeev. "Judicializing Politics: Indian Incongruities." Paper presented at the Interim Meeting of the Comparative Judicial Research Group of the International Political Science Association, Bologna, 1992.

Diamond, Larry. "Three Paradoxes of Democracy." In *The Global Resurgence of Democracy,* ed. Larry Diamond and Marc F. Plattner, 95–107. Baltimore: Johns Hopkins Press, 1993.

Di Federico, Giuseppe. "The Italian Judicial Profession and Its Bureaucratic Setting." *Juridical Review* 21 (1976): 50–62.

———. "La Selezione dei Magistrati: Prospettive Psicologiche" (Selection of magistrates: psychological perspectives). In *Limiti ed Inefficacia della Selezione dei Magistrati,* ed. C. Pedrazzi, 16–21. Milan: Giuffré Editore, 1976.

Dilliard, Irving. "Samuel Chase." In *The Justices of the United States Supreme Court, 1789–1969: Their Lives and Major Opinions,* ed. Leon Friedman and Fred L. Israel, 1:188–89. New York: Chelsea House Publishers, 1969.

Downs, Anthony. *An Economic Theory of Democracy.* New York: Harper and Row Publishers, 1957.

Drewry, Gavin. "Judicial Politics in Britain: Patrolling the Boundaries." *West European Politics* 15 (July 1992): 9–28.

Dubois, Philip L., ed. *The Analysis of Judicial Reform.* Lexington, Mass.: Lexington Books, 1982.

———. "Financing Trial Court Elections: Who Contributes to California Judicial Campaigns?" *Judicature* 70 (June–July 1986): 8–16.

————. *From Ballot to Bench: Judicial Elections and the Quest for Accountability.* Austin: University of Texas Press, 1980.

————. "Voting Cues in Nonpartisan Trial Court Elections: A Multivariate Assessment." *Law and Society Review* 18 (1984): 395–436.

Dumbauld, Edward. *Thomas Jefferson and the Law.* Norman: University of Oklahoma Press, 1978.

Edwards, Drew E. "Judicial Misconduct and Politics in the Federal System: A Proposal for Revising the Judicial Councils Act." *California Law Review* 75 (May 1987): 1071–92.

Ehrmann, Henry. *Comparative Legal Cultures.* Englewood Cliffs, N.J.: Prentice-Hall, 1976.

Ellis, Richard D. *The Jeffersonian Crisis: Courts and Politics in the Young Republic.* New York: W.W. Norton and Company, 1971.

Ely, John Hart. *Democracy and Distrust: A Theory of Judicial Review.* Cambridge: Harvard University Press, 1980.

Fenton, Paul S. "The Scope of the Impeachment Power." *Northwestern University Law Review* 65 (November–December 1970): 719–47.

Fitzpatrick, Collins T. "Misconduct and Disability of Federal Judges: The Unreported Informal Responses." *Judicature* 71 (February–March 1988): 282–83.

Flanders, Steven. "Judicial Discipline, Criminal Prosecution and Impeachment." *Justice System Journal* 11 (Winter 1986): 394–99.

Frank, Jerome. *Courts on Trial: Myth and Reality in American Justice.* Princeton, N.J.: Princeton University Press, 1949.

Friedman, Leon, and Fred L. Israel, eds. *The Justices of the United States Supreme Court, 1789–1969: Their Lives and Major Opinions.* New York: Chelsea House Publishers, 1969.

Galligan, Brian. "Judicial Activism in Australia." In *Judicial Activism in Comparative Perspective,* ed. Kenneth M. Holland, 70–89. London: Macmillan, 1991.

———— and David R. Slater. "Judicial Intrusion into the Australian Cabinet." Paper presented at the Interim Meeting of the Comparative Judicial Politics Research Group of the International Political Science Association, Bologna, 1992.

Gamarra, Eduardo. *The System of Justice in Bolivia: An Institutional Analysis.* Miami, Fla.: Center for the Administration of Justice, 1991.

Gardiner, John A. "Preventing Judicial Misconduct: Defining the Role of Conduct Organizations." *Judicature* 70 (August–September 1986): 113–21.

Gerhardt, Michael J. "The Constitutional Limits to Impeachment and Its Alternatives." *Texas Law Review* 68 (November 1989): 2–104.

Gillespie, Charles Guy. "Democratic Consolidation in the Southern Cone." *Third World Quarterly* 11 (April 1989): 92–113.

Glick, Henry R., and Craig F. Emmert. "Stability and Change: Characteristics of State Supreme Court Justices." *Judicature* 70 (August–September 1986): 107–12.

Gould, Carol C. *Rethinking Democracy: Freedom and Social Cooperation in Politics, Economy and Society.* Cambridge: Cambridge University Press, 1988.

Griffin, Kenyon N., and Michael J. Horan. "Patterns of Voting Behavior in Judicial Retention Elections for Supreme Court Justices in Wyoming." *Judicature* 67 (August 1983): 68–77.

Griffith, J. A. G. *The Politics of the Judiciary.* London: Fontana Press, 1991.

Grossman, Joel B., and Austin Sarat. "Political Culture and Judicial Research." *Washington University Law Quarterly* 2 (1971): 192–98.

Guarnieri, Carlo. *Magistratura e Politica in Italia* (Magistrates and politics in Italy). Bologna: Società Editrice Il Mulino, 1992.

Hall, William K., and Larry T. Aspin. "What Twenty Years of Judicial Retention Elections Have Told Us." *Judicature* 70 (April–May 1987): 340–47.

Hamilton, Alexander. *Federalist Nos. 65, 78, and 79.* New York: Modern Library, 1969.

Henderson, Phillip G. "Marshall Versus Jefferson: Politics and the Federal Judiciary in the Early Republic." *Michigan Journal of Political Science* 11 (1981): 42–68.

Hine, David. *Governing Italy: The Politics of Bargained Pluralism.* Oxford: Clarendon Press, 1993.

Hoelzel, William E. "No Easy Answers: A Report on the National Conference for Judicial Conduct Organizations." *Judicature* 64 (December–January 1981): 279–84.

Hojnacki, Marie, and Lawrence Baum. "Choosing Judicial Candidates How Voters Expain Their Decisions." *Judicature* 75 (April–May 1992): 300–309.

Holdsworth, William. *A History of English Law.* London: Sweet and Maxwell, 1956.

Holland, Kenneth M., ed. *Judicial Activism in Comparative Perspective.* London: Macmillan, 1991.

Holloman, John H. III. "The Judicial Reform Act: History, Analysis and Comment." *Law and Contemporary Problems* 35 (Winter 1970): 128–50.

"I Giudici Piacono Tre Volte Tanto" (The judges are suited three more times). *Corriere della Sera,* 5 August 1993, 16.

Jackson, Donald W., and James W. Riddlesperger, Jr. "Money and Politics in Judicial Elections: The 1988 Election of the Chief Justice of the Texas Supreme Court." *Judicature* 74 (December–January 1991): 184–89.

Jackson, Donald W., and C. Neal Tate, eds. *Comparative Judicial Review and Public Policy.* Westport, Conn.: Greenwood Press, 1992.

Jewell, R. E. C. *British Constitution.* London: Hodder and Stoughton, 1975.

Johnson, Allen, and Dumas Malone, eds. *Dictionary of American Biography.* New York: Charles Scribner's Sons, 1930.

Johnson, Herbert A. *Foundations of Power: John Marshall, 1801–15.* New York: Macmillan Publishing Co., 1981.

Judicial Appointments: The Lord Chancellor's Policies and Procedures. London: HMSO, 1986.

Kales, Albert. *Unpopular Government in the United States.* Chicago: University of Chicago Press, 1914.

Katz, Alan N., ed. *Legal Traditions and Systems.* New York: Greenwood Press, 1986.

Kaufman, Irving R. "Lions or Jackals: The Function of a Code of Judicial Ethics." *Law and Contemporary Problems* 35 (Winter 1970): 3–8.

Kenyon, J. P. *The Stuart Constitution.* Cambridge: Cambridge University Press, 1986.

Kiralfy, A. K. R. *Potter's Historical Introduction to English Law and Its Institutions.* London: Sweet and Maxwell, 1958.

Kiser, Edgar, and Yoram Barzel. "The Origins of Democracy in England." *Rationality and Society* 3 (October 1991): 396–422.

Kommers, Donald P. *The Constitutional Jurisprudence of the Federal Republic of Germany.* Durham, N.C.: Duke University Press, 1989.

Lafon, Jacqueline Lucienne. "The Judicial Career in France: Theory and Practice under the Fifth Republic." *Judicature* 75 (August–September 1991): 97–106.

———. "La Judicialisation de la Politique en France." *International Political Science Review* 15 (April 1994): 135–42.

Landfried, Christine. "Judicial Policy-Making in Germany: The Federal Constitutional Court." *West European Politics* 15 (July 1992): 50–67.

La Palombara, Joseph. *Democracy Italian Style.* New Haven: Yale University Press, 1987.

La Rocca, Guy de. "Le Conseil Supérieur de la Magistrature: Constitutional de la République Française: Loi du 27 Octobre 1946" (The Superior Council of the Magistrature: Constitution of the French Republic, law of 27 October 1946). Thesis, Paris, 1948.

Lawson, Stephanie. "Conceptual Issues in the Comparative Study of Regime Change and Democratization." *Comparative Politics* 25 (January 1993): 183–206.

Lijphart, Arend. "The Comparable-Cases Strategy in Comparative Research." *Comparative Political Studies* 8 (July 1975): 158–77.

———. "Comparative Politics and the Comparative Method." *American Political Science Review* 65 (September 1971): 682–93.

———. *Democracies: Patterns of Majoritarian and Consensus Government in Twenty-One Countries.* New Haven: Yale University Press, 1984.

Lillich, Richard B. "The Chase Impeachment." *American Journal of Legal History* 4 (January 1960): 46–60.

Linz, Juan J., and Alfred Stepan, eds. *The Breakdown of Democratic Regimes.* Baltimore, Md.: Johns Hopkins University Press, 1978.

Lipset, Seymour Martin. *Political Man: The Social Bases of Politics.* Garden City, N.J.: Anchor Books, 1963.

Lois nouvelles analysées et expliquées et Revue des travaux législatifs, 2nd année (New laws analyzed and explained and review of legislative work, 2nd year). Paris: Bureau du Recueil, 1883.

Lovrich, Nicholas P., John C. Pierce, and Charles H. Sheldon. "Citizen Knowledge and Voting in Judicial Elections." *Judicature* 73 (June–July 1989): 28–33.

Lubet, Steven. *Beyond Reproach: Ethical Restrictions on the Extrajudicial Activities of State and Federal Judges.* Chicago: American Judicature Society, 1984.

———. "Judicial Ethics and Private Lives." *Northwestern University Law Review* 79 (February 1985): 983–1008.

———. "Participation by Judges in Civic and Charitable Activities: What Are the Limits?" *Judicature* 69 (August–September 1985): 68–76.

McDowell, Gary L. "The Moral Wish as Father to Constitutional Thought: Constitutional Fate." *Louisiana Law Review* 45 (January 1985): 831–62.

McFadden, Patrick M. *Electing Justice: The Law and Ethics of Judicial Elections Campaigns.* Chicago: American Judicature Society, 1990.

"Magistratopoli, Quando Arriverà il Momento dell'Inchiesta 'Toghe Pulite' " (Magistrate-city, when the moment arrives for "clean robes" investigation). *Corriere della Sera,* 14 April 1993, 5.

Mahler, Gregory S. *Comparative Politics: An Institutional and Cross-National Approach.* Englewood Cliffs, N.J.: Prentice-Hall, 1992.

Manchester, A. H. *Modern Legal History of England and Wales.* London: Butterworths, 1980.

Mandel, Michael. *The Charter of Rights and the Legalization of Politics in Canada.* Toronto: Wall & Thompson, 1989.

Manheim, Jarol B., and Richard C. Rich. *Empirical Political Analysis: Research Methods in Political Science.* New York: Longman, 1991.

Marsh, James G., and Johan P. Olsen. "The New Institutionalism: Organizational Factors in Political Life." *American Political Science Review* 78 (September 1984): 734–49.

Mathias, Sara. *Electing Justice: A Handbook of Judicial Elections Reforms.* Chicago: American Judicature Society, 1990.

Maxman, Melissa H. "In Defense of the Constitution's Judicial Impeachment Standard." *Michigan Law Review* 86 (November 1987): 420–63.

Mény, Yves. *Government and Politics in Western Europe: Britain, France, Italy and West Germany.* Oxford: Oxford University Press, 1990.

Micali, Giovanni. "Per un Contributo all'Elaborazatione del Codice Disciplinare dei Magistrati" (A contribution to elaborate the disciplinary code of the magistrates). *Giurisprudenza Italiana* 163, pt. 4 (April 1991): 145–49.

Miller, Benjamin K. "Assessing the Functions of Judicial Conduct Organizations." *Judicature* 75 (June–July 1991): 16–19.

"Mob Prosecutor to Aid in Inquiry." *New York Times,* 5 September 1993, Y-10.

Montesquieu, Baron Charles de. *The Spirit of the Laws.* Trans. Thomas Nugent. New York: Hafner Publishing Co., 1949.

Moog, Robert. "Campaign Financing for North Carolina's Appellate Courts." *Judicature* 76 (August–September 1992): 68–76.

Morgan, Peter W. "The Appearance of Propriety: Ethics Reform and the Blifil Paradoxes." *Stanford Law Review* 44 (January 1992): 593–621.

Morton, F. L. "Judicial Activism in France." In *Judicial Activism in Comparative Perspective,* ed. Kenneth M. Holland, 133–53. London: Macmillan, 1991.

Murphy, Bruce Allen. *Fortas: The Rise and Ruin of a Supreme Court Justice.* New York: William Morrow, 1988.

Negri, Guglielmo. *Il Quadro Costitutionale: Tempi e Istituti della Libertà* (The constitutional picture: times and institutions of liberty). Rome: Giuffré Editore, 1984.

Nicholson, Marlene Arnold, and Bradley Scott Weiss. "Funding Judicial Campaigns in the Circuit Court of Cook County." *Judicature* 70 (June–July 1986): 17–26.

O'Connor, Alice, and Mary L. Henze. *"During Good Behavior": Judicial Independence and Accountability.* Washington: The Jefferson Foundation, 1984.

O'Donnell, Guillermo, Philippe C. Schmitter, and Laurence Whitehead, eds. *Transitions from Authoritarian Rule: Comparative Perspectives.* Baltimore, Md.: Johns Hopkins University Press, 1991.

Olson, Mancur. "Dictatorship, Democracy and Development." *American Political Science Review* 87 (September 1993): 567–76.

Palazzolo, Salvatore. "Composizione ed Elezione del Consiglio Superiore della Magistratura" (Composition and election of the Superior Council of the Magistrature). *Giurisprudenza Italiana* 143, pt. 4 (April 1991): 166.

Pannick, David. *Judges.* Oxford: Oxford University Press, 1987.

Pedrazzi, C., ed. *Limiti ed Inefficacia della Selezione dei Magistrati* (Limits and ineffectiveness of the selection of magistrates). Milan: Guiffré Editore, 1976.

Pepin et Scherer. *Organisation judiciaire et preparation a l'examen professionnel d'entree dans la magistrature* (Judicial organization and preparation for the professional entrance exam for the magistrature). Paris, 1950.

Perlstein, Jolanta Juszkiewicz, and Nathan Goldman, "Judicial Disciplinary Commissions: A New Approach to the Discipline and Removal of State Judges." In *The Analysis of Judicial Reform,* ed. Philip L. Dubois, 93–106. Lexington, Mass: Lexington Books, 1982.

Perry, Michael J. *The Constitution, the Courts and Human Rights.* New Haven: Yale University Press, 1982.

Phillips, O. Hood, and A. H. Hudson. *O. Hood Phillips' First Book of English Law.* London: Sweet and Maxwell, 1988.

Pica, Georges, and Liane Cobert. *Le Cour de Cassation, Que sais-je?* (The Court of Cassation, what do I know?). Paris: P.U.F., 1986.

Pizzorusso, Alessandro. "Poteri del CSM e Potere del Presidente del CSM circa la Formazione e la Modificazione dell-Ordine del Giorno delle Sedute" (Powers of the CSM and power of the president of the CSM in the formation and modification of the order of the day's sitting). *Questione Giustizia* (1985): 727.

———. *Sistema Istituzionale del Diritto Pubblico Italiano* (Institutional system of Italian public law). Naples: Jovene Editore, 1988.

———, V. Zagrebelsky, and V. Carbone, eds. *Commentario della Costituzione: Art. 108–110* (Commentary on the Constitution: Articles 108–110). Bologna: Zanichelli Editore, 1992.

Plucknett, T. F. T. *Studies in English Legal History.* London: Hambledon Press, 1983.

Preuss, Ulrich. "Aus dem Geiste des Konsenses: Zur Rechtsprechung des Bundesverfassungsgerichts" (From the spirit of consensus: legal discourse of the Constitutional Court). *Merkur* (1987): 1–12.

Proceedings in the Senate Preliminary to the Trial of Charles Swayne, Judge of the District Court of the United States in and for the Northern District of Florida, upon the Articles of Impeachment Exhibited by the House of Representatives. Washington: U.S. Government Printing Office, 1905.

Przeworski, Adam. "Some Problems in the Study of the Transition to Democracy." In *Transitions from Authoritarian Rule: Comparative Perspectives,* ed. Guillermo O'Donnell, Philippe C. Schmitter, and Laurence Whitehead, 47–63. Baltimore, Md.: Johns Hopkins University Press, 1991.

———, and Henry Teune. *The Logic of Comparative Social Inquiry.* Malabar, Fla.: Robert E. Krieger Publishing Company, 1970.

Putnam, Robert. *Making Democracy Work: Civic Traditions in Modern Italy.* Princeton: Princeton University Press, 1993.

Quaderni del Consiglio Superiori della Magistratura, *Manuale dell'Udienza Disciplinare: Massime della Sezione Disciplinare dal 1 Gennairo al 31 Dicembre 1991* (Manual for disciplinary audiences: major decisions from January 1 to December 31, 1991). Vol. 7 (October 1992): 40.

"Quaranta Giudici sotto Inchiesta" (Forty judges under investigation). *Italia,* 19 March 1993, 8.

Ragin, Charles C. *The Comparative Method: Moving Beyond Qualitative and Quantitative Strategies.* Berkeley: University of California Press, 1987.

Rehnquist, William H. *Grand Inquests: The Historic Impeachments of Justice Samuel Chase and President Andrew Johnson.* New York: William Morrow, 1992.

———. "Sense and Nonsense about Judicial Ethics." *Record* 28 (November 1973): 694–713.

Ricard, Thierry. *Le Conseil Superiéur de la Magistrature, Que sais-je?* (The Superior Council of the Magistrature, what do I know?). Paris: P.U.F., 1991.

Rieger, Carol T. "The Judicial Councils Reform and Judicial Conduct and Disability Act: Will Judges Judge Judges?" *Emory Law Journal* 37 (Winter 1988): 45–97.

Rodotá, Carla. *La Corte Costituzionale: Come e chi Garantisce il Pieno Respetto della Nostra Costituzione?* (The Constitutional Court: how and who guarantees the fullness of our constitution?). Rome: Editori Riuniti, 1986.

Rosenbaum, Judith. *Practices and Procedures of State Judicial Conduct Organizations.* Chicago: American Judicature Society, 1990.

Roskell, J. S. *The Impeachment of Michael de la Pole, Earl of Suffolk in 1386: In the Context of the Reign of Richard II.* Manchester: Manchester University Press, 1984.

Rousselet, Marcel. *Histoire de la magistrature Française des origines à nos jours* (History of the French magistrature, origins to our days). Paris: Plon, 1957.

Royer, Jean-Pierre. *La société judiciare depuis le xviii siècle* (The society of judges after the eighteenth century). Paris: P.U.F., 1979.

Sangmpam, S. N. "Overpoliticized State and Democratization: A Theoretical Model." *Comparative Politics* 24 (July 1992): 401–18.

Sartori, Giovanni. "Concept Misinformation in Comparative Politics." *American Political Science Review* 6 (December 1970): 1033–53.

———. *The Theory of Democracy Revisited*. Chatham, N.J.: Chatham House, 1987.

Schemo, Diane Jean. "Seeking Leniency, Wachtler Blames Adversaries." *New York Times,* 5 September 1993, Y-15.

Schmidhauser, John R. "Alternative Conceptual Frameworks in Comparative Cross-National Legal and Judicial Research." In *Comparative Judicial Systems: Challenging Frontiers in Conceptual and Empirical Analysis,* ed. John R. Schmidhauser, 1–38. London: Butterworths, 1989.

———. "Introduction: The Impact of Political Change upon Law, Courts and Judicial Elites." *International Political Science Review* 13 (July 1992): 223–34.

Schmitter, Phillippe C., and Terry Lynn Karl. "What Democracy Is . . . and Is Not." In *The Global Resurgence of Democracy,* ed. Larry Diamond and Marc F. Plattner, 39–52. Baltimore, Md.: Johns Hopkins University Press, 1993.

Senese, Salvatore. "Il Governo della Magistratura in Italia Oggi" (The government of magistrates in Italy today). In *Governo e Autogoverno della Magistratura nell Europa Occidentale,* ed. Pier Luigi Zanchetta, 19–34. Milan: Franco Angeli, 1987.

———. "La Formazione dei Magistrati in Europa ed il Ruolo dei Sindacati e delle Associazione Professionale: Quale Formazione, per quale Giustizia in quale Società?" (The socialization of magistrates in Europe and the role of unions and professional associations: what socialization, for what justice in what society?). *Il Foro Italiano* 116, pt. 5 (November 1991): 538.

Shaman, Jeffery M., Steven Lubet, and James J. Alfini. "The 1990 Code of Judicial Conduct: An Overview." *Judicature* 74 (June–July 1990): 21–27.

Shapiro, Martin. *Courts: A Comparative and Political Analysis*. Chicago: University of Chicago Press, 1981.

———. "The Juridicalization of Politics in the United States." *International Political Science Review* 15 (April 1994): 101–12.

Sherry, Suzanna. "Issue Manipulation by the Berger Court: Saving the Community from Itself." *Minnesota Law Review* 70 (February 1986): 611–63.

Shetreet, Simon. *Judges on Trial: A Study of the Appointment and Accountability of the English Judiciary*. Amsterdam: North Holland Publishing Company, 1976.

"Sí, il CSM Ha Tollerator Inefficienze e Timidezze." *La Republilica,* 21 August 1993.

Skocpol, Theda. *Vision and Method in Historical Sociology*. Cambridge: Cambridge University Press, 1984.

Smith, Nancy J., and Julie Garmel. "Judicial Election and Selection Procedures Challenged under the Voting Rights Act." *Judicature* 76 (October–November 1992): 154–57.

Smith, Roger M. "Political Jurisprudence, the 'New Institutionalism,' and the Future of Public Law." *American Political Science Review* 82 (March 1988): 89–108.

Stevens, Robert. *Law and Politics: The House of Lords as a Judicial Body, 1800–1976.* Chapel Hill: University of North Carolina Press, 1978.

Stone, Alec. *The Birth of Judicial Politics in France: The Constitutional Council in Comparative Perspective*. New York: Oxford University Press, 1992.

Tate, C. Neal. "Courts and Crisis Regimes: A Theory Sketch with Asian Case Studies." *Political Research Quarterly* 46 (June 1993): 311–38.

———. "Recruitment to the British Appellate Judiciary, 1876–1972: Causal Models." *International Political Science Review* 13 (July 1992): 263–64.

Ten Broek, Jacobus. "Partisan Politics and Federal Judgeship Impeachment Since 1903." *Minnesota Law Review* 23 (1939): 185–204.

Tesauro, Alfonso. *Manuale di Diritto Pubblico* (Manual of public law). Naples: Edizioni Scientifiche Italiane, 1973.

Trial of John Pickering, Judge of the New Hampshire District, on a Charge Exhibited to the Senate of the United States, for High Crimes and Misdemeanors. S. Doc. 876 (1804).

Trial of Samuel Chase, An Associate Justice of the Supreme Court of the United States. Taken in short-hand by Samuel H. Smith and Thomas Lloyd. Washington, D.C.: Samuel H. Smith, 1805.

Turner, Lynn. "The Impeachment of John Pickering." *American Historical Review* 65 (April 1949): 496–505.

Tushnet, Mark. *Red, White and Blue: A Critical Analysis of Constitutional Law.* Cambridge: Harvard University Press, 1988.

UN Commission on Human Rights, Subcommission on Prevention of Discrimination and Protection of Minorities. "Basic Principles on the Independence of the Judiciary." 4 July 1988.

Urofsky, Melvin I., ed. *American Constitutional and Legal History.* New York: Alfred A. Knopf, 1989.

Valentino, Nino. *Il Presidente della Repubblica: Maestro di Corte or Tribune del Popolo?* (President of the Republic: teacher of the court or tribune of the people?) Rome: Editalia, 1992.

Van Koppen, Peter J. "Judicial Policy-Making in the Netherlands: The Case-by-Case Method." *West European Politics* 15 (July 1992): 80–92.

Van Tassel, Emily Field. *Why Judges Resign: Influences on Federal Judicial Service, 1789 to 1992.* Washington: Federal Judicial History Office and Federal Judicial Center, 1993.

Verougstraete, Ivan. "Judicial Politics in Belgium." *West European Politics* 15 (July 1992): 93–108.

Volcansek, Mary L. "Codes of Judicial Ethics: Do They Affect Judges' View of Proper Off-the-Bench Behavior?" *American Business Law Journal* 17 (Winter 1980): 493–505.

———. *Judicial Impeachment: None Called for Justice.* Chicago: University of Illinois Press, 1993.

———. "The Judicial Role in Italy: Independence, Impartiality and Legitimacy." *Judicature* 73 (April–May 1990): 322–27.

———, ed. *Judicial Politics and Policy-Making in Western Europe.* London: Frank Cass & Co., 1992.

Volcansek, Mary L., and Jacqueline Lucienne Lafon. *Judicial Selection: The Cross-Evolution of French and American Practices.* Westport, Conn.: Greenwood Press, 1988.

Wade, E. C. S., and G. Godfrey Phillips. *Constitutional Law*. London: Longmans, 1960.

Waltman, Jerold L. "Judicial Activism in England." In *Judicial Activism in Comparative Perspective*, ed. Kenneth M. Holland, 33–52. London: Macmillan, 1991.

Warrick, Lyle. *Judicial Selection in the United States: A Compendium of Provisions*. Chicago: American Judicature Society, 1993.

Whitehead, Laurence. "International Aspects of Democratization." In *Transitions from Authoritarian Rule: Comparative Perspectives*, ed. Guillermo O'Donnell, Philippe C. Schmitter, and Laurence Whitehead, Baltimore, 3–46. Baltimore, Md.: Johns Hopkins University Press, 1991.

Wood, Gordon S. *The Creation of the American Republic, 1776–1787*. Chapel Hill: University of North Carolina Press, 1969.

Yackle, Larry W. "Choosing Judges the Democratic Way." *Boston University Law Review* 69 (March 1989): 273–328.

Zanchetta, Pier Luigi, ed. *Governo e Autogoverno della Magistratura nell'Europa Occidentale* (Government and self-government of the magistrature in Western Europe). Milan: Franco Angeli, 1987.

Index

About the Authors

Mary L. Volcansek is professor and chair of political science at Florida International University, where she has been since completing her Ph.D. in political science from Texas Tech University in 1973. She has written *Judicial Politics in Europe* (1986) and *Judicial Impeachment* (1993), coauthored with Jacqueline Lafon *Judicial Selection: The Cross-Evolution of French and American Practices* (1988), and edited *Judicial Politics and Policy-Making in Western Europe* (1992). She has also published a number of articles and book chapters on judicial behavior and judicial politics in the United States and Europe.

Maria Elisabetta de Franciscis is assistant professor of political science at Università di Napoli, Federico II. She received her *laurea* there in 1979 and her M.A. and Ph.D. in political science from the University of Connecticut. She has published *Italy and the Vatican* (1989) and a number of articles on Italian politics and law and on the U.S. political system, in both the United States and Italy.

Jacqueline Lucienne Lafon is asssociate professor of law at Université de Paris, XI, where she has also served as associate dean. Her doctorate is from the Sorbonne. She is the author of *Les Députés du Commerce et l'Ordonnance de mar 1673* and *Juges et Consuls: À la recherche d'un statut dans la France d'Ancien Régime* and coauthor of *Judicial Selection: The Cross-Evolution of French and American Practices*. She has also published articles in *Judicature, International Political Science Review, Etudes d'Histoire du Droit Parisien,* and *Revue Historique de Droit Français et Etranger*.